Dolls' House
Fireplaces & Stoves

Dolls' House Fireplaces & Stoves

Patricia King

Guild of Master Craftsman Publications Ltd

First published 1999 by
Guild of Master Craftsman Publications Ltd,
166 High Street, Lewes,
East Sussex, BN7 1XU

ISBN 1 86108 105 7

Photographs by Steve Hawkins

Line drawings by Roderick King

Designed by Ed White
Cover designed by Wheelhouse Design

Typefaces: Regular Joe and Bembo

Colour reproduction by Job Color srl – Gorle (BG) – Italy
Printed by Sun Fung Offset Binding Co Ltd

I would like to dedicate this book to Ryan, newly minted
and already smart as a new penny...

and to thank Roderick, my friend, my son and my illustrator, for
his skill and innovation, and his GRATE illustrations...

and Lindy Dunlop for patiently tidying up all the loose ends I leave her.

NOTE ON BRAND NAMES

Specific brand names have been used purely to identify particular shapes of packaging. The brand itself is not important, and any other packaging or items of similar shape can be substituted.

Contents

3 COOKING STOVES

4 PORTABLE HEATERS

5 COAL HODS, FIRE IRONS AND FIREGUARDS

Introduction

Hobbies are wonderful aren't they? Perhaps I am biased, but I think dolls' housing is one of the best hobbies you can have. You can create your own little world where everything is as you wish it to be, and it incorporates so many other pursuits. You can own beautiful things in miniature which you would never be able to afford in real size, even if you had a place to put them, and once you have acquired them you can arrange them without the usual housework. You can even indulge an interest in antiques, buying them in miniature.

Buying dolls' house bits and pieces is quite a pursuit in itself. When you visit a town you haven't been to before, what is more natural than to find the nearest dolls' house shop to browse in and chat with fellow enthusiasts, and possibly find a treasure to buy as a souvenir. And you really are doing friends and family a favour having such a hobby because they can always buy or make you something for the dolls' house for birthday or Christmas presents!

Nostalgia can play a large part in the dolls' house world. In your own little house you can go back to times of old when life seemed more gracious, and people it with beautifully dressed occupants who will quickly take on roles in the household. You'll find yourself naming them and acquiring an extra family with whimsical histories!

Then there's the enjoyment and challenge of making things. I find it very rewarding if I succeed in making a convincing replica in miniature, and modelling my way does not require a lot of room or expense. Using found bits and pieces to make furniture and effects brings about another aspect of the hobby, a built-in excuse to go to jumble and boot sales to find likely makings. You never know what you will find there and often it is the unexpected buy that inspires a new creation: a picture frame you picked up for a few pence may become your favourite fireplace.

So if you need a bolt hole to escape your everyday cares, to give you a dream and a multi-faceted hobby, make it dolls' housing. You can have a 'grate' time with it.

CHAPTER 1
MATERIALS AND TECHNIQUES

Tools and Safety

It is a bit cheeky, I feel, for me to advise you about tools. If I was more confident in using tools, I'm sure I would never have developed ways of making things that cut out the need for them.

You don't need a fully-equipped workshop and a large assortment of tools for modelling with found objects: it is essentially a tabletop hobby and the minimum of tools will see you through.

Here is the short list of tools that I find essential:

- Biggish board to keep things together and to carry them to and fro.
- Self-healing cutting board with a printed grid to cut on and to help in working out angles.
- Break-off craft knives which are cheap and give you lots of fresh cutting blades.
- Steel ruler, to give a precise cutting edge.
- Pliers, both long-nosed and miniature.
- Mini drill: an electric drill is a nice luxury, but you will need goggles.
- Modellers' vice (all my vices are small ones). No! They hold things.
- Emery boards, for manicuring fingernails, are the perfect shape for getting into corners.
- Exacto saw and spare blades.
- Paper punch for making holes.
- Scissors, small and large. Pinking shears are also handy.
- Wire cutters: you can get nice, small ones.
- Compass: use the point to make small holes or rivets.
- Clothes pegs to grip things when you run out of hands.
- Pencils, paintbrushes and Chinagraph pencils: a Chinagraph pencil will write on shiny surfaces, and is sharper than an eyebrow pencil.
- Glue gun for finishing the job. Don't get one that is too small – they do not get hot enough to do a good job.

Paints

It's surprising how a coat of paint unites all the different parts in a piece. There are many types available, and on the whole you're best using what you find easiest and what you have in stock.

Note that paints do not cover white card well, so for a better finish use either black card or grey card painted black where this is required – do not attempt to paint white card.

WATERCOLOURS

I list these first because most families have a paintbox around, and they will do most painting jobs for you. When you have coloured your object, give it a coat or two of varnish then wash the brush immediately in nail varnish remover.

Watercolour can be persuaded to cover shiny surfaces if you drag your brush over a bar of toilet soap before dipping it in the colour.

ACRYLICS

Acrylic paints can do everything that watercolours can, will paint over shiny surfaces, give a better cover than watercolours, and a lovely eggshell finish. But their great advantage is that the shaped tray from the six-tube packaging can be made into a wonderful urinal!

EMULSION

Emulsion paints give a very good finish on stone or marble surfaces. They are also useful for giving a sheer coverage on light areas.

CELLULOSE CAR SPRAY AND MODELLERS' PAINTS

I use car spray and modellers' paints for most models as they give a good, even coat and shine without clogging up and obscuring the fine details of the piece. These paints must be used outside as they give off toxic fumes, but you can get cheap packets of paper masks at car supplies shops. (If you inhale they may kill you, but they will give you a good finish!)

ENAMELS

I find enamels messy and overly thick, but they do give a good cover, and spray enamels can be very useful. Do not use enamel and cellulose spray paints over one another as they will come out in blotches!

SPRAY DIFFUSER

In the foreground of Fig 1.2 is a little spray diffuser. These are available, very reasonably, from art supplies shops, and can be used with watercolours and acrylics to give an air-brushed effect.

Materials

It's not a bounden rule that if you like modelling with found objects you have to be a jumble and car boot sale addict, but where are you going to get your materials from if you're not? When you want to make something in a hurry, you really need to have a stock of useful bits and pieces so you can just reach for the right twiddly bit without interruption. Like as not, the bit you want will come from a jewellery finding, used either whole or cut up. If you've amassed this sort of thing you're halfway there. (Mind you, if you live anywhere within a five-mile radius of me, you may as well forget it: ten to one I'll have been to the local boot sale before you and gathered everything that has modelling potential!)

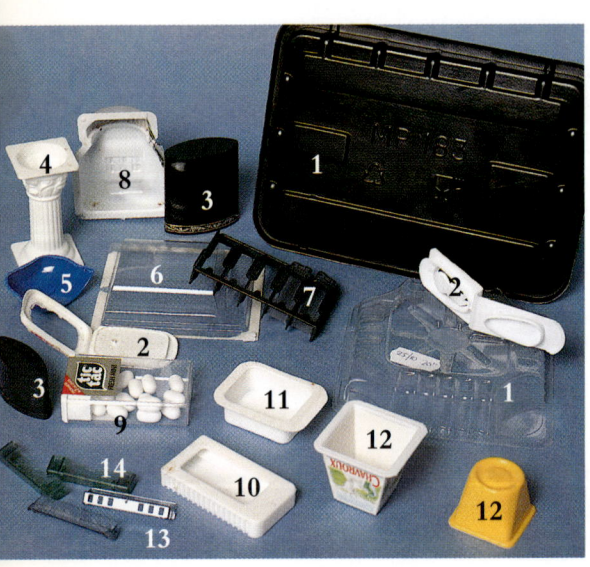

1 Plastic supermarket pack
2 Pourer from fruit juice carton
3 Elliptical make-up top
4 Cake pillar
5 Eye bath
6 Bubble packs
7 Gillette razor holder
8 Single portion Nutella tub
9 tic tac box
10 Safety razor blades, five-pack
11 Single portion butter tub
12 Single portion goat's cheese
13 Hairclip slide
14 Razor blade guards

1   Make-up packaging
2   Single portion pickle tub
3   Airline gin bottle, plastic
4   Single portion jam tub
5   Sweetener pack
6   Single portion Nutella tub
7   Contact lens bubble pack
8   Single portion butter tub

But do not despair! There is always recyclable rubbish. Most people feel there is far too much packaging about; by the time you have unpacked your shopping, you often find you have a larger pile of wrapping than purchases! A lot of this packaging can be useful to the dolls' house modeller.

Look carefully at the small rubbish to see if it contains any useful shapes, either whole or cut up. Bubble packs such as those made to protect batteries, screws, paperclips, razor blades and packs of sweeteners, all make good windows, door panels, stand-up stoves or rounded details that it would be hard to make any other way.

Once you start to examine the ready-made shapes of packaging, the throw-away society becomes your plaything and your world will take on a new dimension. In your search for materials you may go out for coffee and come back clutching the plastic tub your milk came in (to make a loo pedestal), the individual portion butter tub (for a sink or cistern), a straw (for a downpipe) and a sweetener pack for a stove or fireplace. And if your eating excesses lead you to the chemist so much the better . . . You will find a wealth of lovely bubble packs (those for razor blades make wide china sinks, the little round indents in pill packets make very nice hats and aspirin bottles make good stoves) as well as razors (excellent for the wide mouth of an old vacuum cleaner). The list is endless.

Visit an ironmonger if you can and you'll find all sorts of lovely makings. Copper cylinders make good geysers and brass olives transform into saucepans. You'll also find another interesting range of bubble packs covering door handles and the like.

Picture and photo frames make good fireplace surrounds and fenders. You can use the entire frame as it is, or cut the bottom section

off and use it as a fender, and the top section as a surround.

Sections cut from fans can be used to add detail or to create an ornate base for a heater, as I have done with the Fan Heater shown on page 89.

Once you have served your apprenticeship in small rubbish collecting in your own country you are ready to go abroad! I suggest you fly, collecting the miniature drinks bottles from anyone within reach and, if possible, some of the squarish airline dessert dishes (good for fireplace surrounds). On reaching your hotel, gather any courtesy soap, shampoo and shoe cleaner. At breakfast I urge you to try the pâté, the various cheeses, the butter and the jam, all of which come in little throwaway packs different from the ones back home!

Fortunately, all these items are small and don't add up to a huge storage problem. While I do admit such a collection does mount up a bit, the answer to *that* problem is – make something new out of all the blooming rubbish that's cluttering up the place! If you like stoves, here are some ideas . . .

BOTTLES, BRACELETS AND BUCKLES

Bottles, bracelets and buckles are all very useful materials for making stoves. Keeping a look out for likely makings adds a certain zest to your life; you may find makings in the most unlikely places.

There are interesting shapes to be found in courtesy bottles of shampoo, body lotion, mouthwash, paint and plant food and, of course, in miniature drinks bottles. You can use these bottles as they are or, if they are plastic, cut them up and use just the odd curve.

Bracelets and belts (the chain variety) are wonderful: they give you several makings in one find. You can use them for oven plates, doors and makers' nameplates.

Even I have a small vice (who doesn't) and I use it often to straighten a curved link or to bend a link over to form a sill. Incorporating links in your models will give them that wonderful fussy look so beloved by the Edwardians, without much effort.

If you like your doors to have burnished fittings, once you have sprayed the whole stove, wipe over the metal parts with a cotton bud dipped in nail varnish.

Bracelets make very effective fenders. Look out for metal ones (tooled or filigree), open them up and straighten them, then bend either end around to form the desired shape. Add a brass paper clip to each end for a pillar. Link bracelets can also give an interesting look: back them with a piece of card to keep the fender stiff.

Buckles come in every size and shape, and providing you can remove the central strut, they make marvellous tabletops (when filled in), fire surrounds and door frames (as for the Victorian Overmantel and Valor-Perfection Oil Stove on pages 20 and 66).

JEWELLERY FINDINGS

I find myself using the term jewellery finding more often than I should. I hear you cry 'What on earth is a jewellery finding?', and well you may ask. Well, basically, anything I can't think how to describe in any other way. It is often the twiddle you've collected, which will be different from the one I have. It could be a found item or a bought thing: lots of firms sell brooch and earring mountings which you can use either whole or cut up, but I am more likely to use an odd earring or a broken chain that has been given to me. Jewellery findings add a touch of decoration.

The words, 'Is this any good to you?,' are music to the dolls' house modeller's ear, and the words 'jewellery findings' should have the same effect. When you see them, rush to the box of treasures they mark and look for the sorts of findings I have suggested.

Many is the time I have been lost in admiration when shown a beautiful dolls' house piece I couldn't possibly have thought of, and when I ask where the modeller got the idea they reply, 'It's one of yours!'. Well, all I can say is, it may have started with a suggestion of mine, but it's the maker's interpretation that has made it so unique!

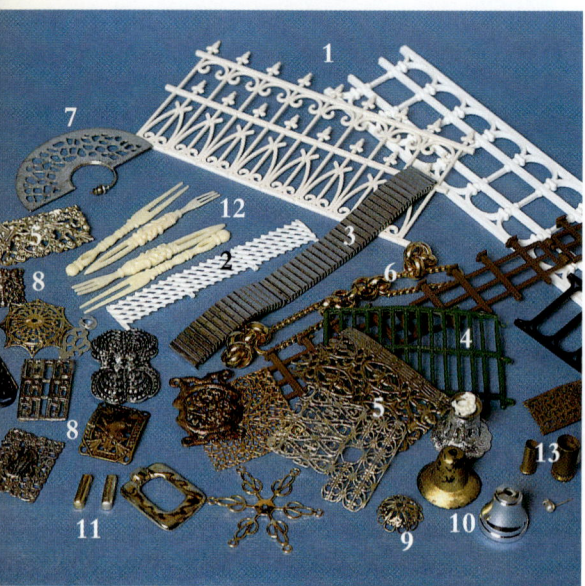

1 Dolls' house banister/balustrade
2 Model railway fencing
3 Metal watch strap
4 Toy zoo fencing
5 Filigree metal jewellery findings
6 Chain links
7 Fan-shaped earring
8 Bracelet or chain belt lozenge
9 Metal bead cap
10 Dress studs
11 Jewellery findings
12 Cocktail forks
13 Brass cartridge cases

Brickwork, Tiles and Fireplace Surrounds

How you treat the surfaces of your fireplaces will have a huge impact on their character and appearance. For a modern finish, simply varnish stripwood and rub it down with light sandpaper. Older styles look better with a dark stain, finished with a coat or two of varnish. Watercolours, acrylics, enamels and cellulose car spray paints can all be used.

BRICKWORK

Alternatively, create a brick or tiled finish. There are modellers I know who make separate, individual bricks for brickwork and I am full of admiration for their work, but if you don't have that dedication, I advocate a short-cut method using foamboard which gives a good result with minimum effort.

Foamboard is available from artists' suppliers, where it can be bought by the sheet. It can be cut easily with a craft knife and has lateral strength which makes it useful for structural components such as walls and floors. Foamboard is actually a sandwich of polystyrene encased in two sheets of light card.

METHOD

1 Mark off the area of foamboard that you want to transform into brickwork, cutting only into the top layer of card.

2 Strip off this top layer to expose the polystyrene and use the craft knife to score in horizontal and vertical lines to outline the bricks. Stagger the vertical lines every other row.

3 Work over these lines with the compass point to widen them and give them an uneven appearance.

4 To colour the bricks, make up a thin mix of watercolours to the colour of black tea and paint over the marked area.

5 Make up your fireplace from this textured material.

An even quicker method is to buy sheets of ready-printed, scale brick paper, which is fairly convincing and can be improved by picking out the odd brick in a different colour.

TILING

Dolls' house suppliers sell a wonderful range of tile papers in scale, but if you want an alternative, look out for giftwrap and postcards with tile designs. A good source for these are art gallery and museum gift shops. Why not go to the source and find a book or catalogue with a picture of the tile you fancy. There are many books on period fireplaces and designers such as William Morris, which contain attractive tile designs. If photocopying the designs does not infringe the copyright terms of the book, take the picture along to a photocopying service with colour facilities and get it reduced to the correct size for your purposes.

It doesn't matter what size the tile is, or even if only one tile is shown. A single tile can be repeated to fill a whole page for about the same cost as a commercial dolls' house sheet. To give a realistic sheen, give the tiles a coat of varnish when they are in place.

INSTALLING A FIREPLACE

Fireplaces are often the focal point of a room, setting the period and providing a showcase for all sorts of knick-knacks, but some of them, notably kitchen ranges, AGAs and inglenooks, need to be set back. This presents a problem if you are installing a fireplace in a ready-made dolls' house with a plain wall and no alcove built in! If you are making a purpose-built room there is no problem – you can recess a chimney area from the start – but the idea of cutting a hole from the wall of an existing dolls' house may not appeal. Even if you are brave enough to go ahead, it will leave you with a chimney area that sticks out, so here are a couple of ideas to get around the problem.

1 Cheat! This method works for domestic-style fireplaces, but is not suitable for ranges. Build your fireplace frame forward, and when you cut out the area to take the grate, back it with a piece of dark paper stuck to the real wall. Put a fireguard or a bowl of dried flowers in front of the hole and no-one will know the difference. (If a friend should notice, have no more to do with them!)

2 Build a false back wall in order to box the fireplace. This will create a recess, though it will lessen the space in your room. However, you can get the best of both worlds if you simply bring forward a wall on either side of the fireplace, keeping it just deep enough to house the stove. This will create three recesses: the central one to take the fireplace and the recesses either side to house a sink or dresser or whatever. Block in the area above the mantelpiece with a false wall.

FIREPLACE SURROUNDS

Often a fireplace is the first thing people need to put in a dolls' house; they buy a house which is complete inside except for the fireplace. Something has to be done, but it need not be elaborate.

If you want to keep it simple, almost any little box on its side will serve the purpose, but you could move on to a slightly more realistic effect by using small picture frames, and there really is a marvellous choice – elaborate and simple, round and rectangular can be found. You can even put one frame inside another to give a mantelpiece and fire surround. If you can't be bothered with grate detail (sorry!), stick a brooch across the opening as an attractive firescreen.

Getting more realistic involves a little more work. You can cut the bottom inch or so off the frame and bring this piece forward to make a step or fender. The space thus created then needs to be filled in with card. But if you keep an eye out for useful shapes, there is sweet possibility in bubble packs. The Canderel handbag pack, for instance, makes a lovely fireplace frame with the recess already built-in.

Now you are getting more ambitious, perhaps you would like to look at some other ideas . . .

CHAPTER 2
FIXED FIREPLACES

Victorian Overmantel

The fireplace usually sets the tone of the whole room and for sheer drama this Victorian Overmantel is hard to beat. It also has the advantage of display space for lots of knick-knacks.

MATERIALS

Small picture frames x 2
Sections from dolls'
     house balustrade
Child's fancy hairslide
Stick-on furniture decoration,
     curlicue
Lolly mould or small, curved
     bubble pack
Brass buckle
Turned dolls' house banister
Handbag mirror
Decorative beads
     (perhaps 2 small and 2 big)
Pins x 2
Sheet of tiles, to scale
Firm card
Balsa wood
Long jewellery findings x 2

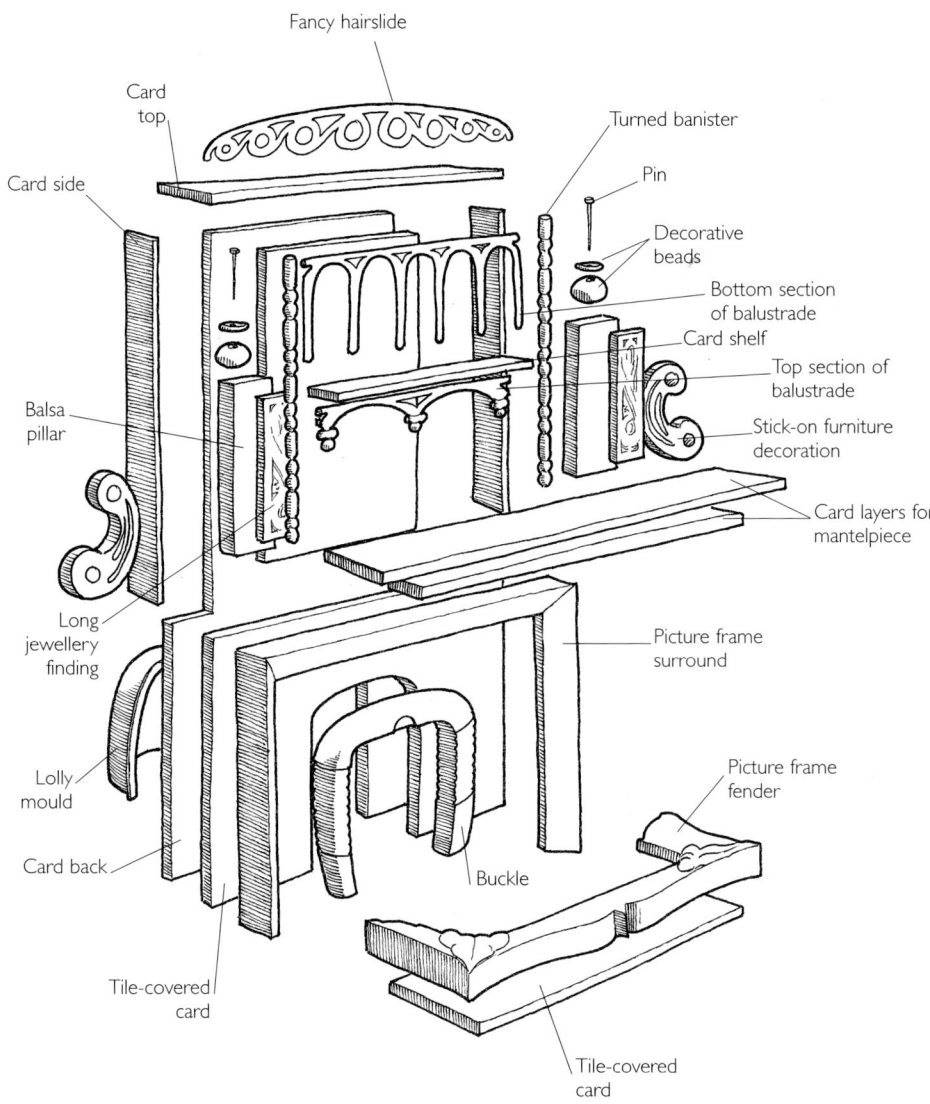

Fancy hairslide

Card top

Card side

Turned banister

Pin

Decorative beads

Bottom section of balustrade

Card shelf

Top section of balustrade

Balsa pillar

Stick-on furniture decoration

Card layers for mantelpiece

Long jewellery finding

Picture frame surround

Picture frame fender

Lolly mould

Card back

Buckle

Tile-covered card

Tile-covered card

METHOD

1 Cut the bottom off one of the picture frames and use the larger part as the fireplace surround.

2 Cut a small section from the bottom of the second frame and use this to form a fender.

3 Cut card to fit inside the fireplace surround and fender.

4 Lay the buckle on the card back, trace around the inside and cut out a hole. Cover both card pieces with the tile sheet and glue the buckle over the hole to frame it. Put these two card pieces to one side.

5 Paint the lolly mould or bubble pack black and then glue it behind the hole as a chimney breast.

6 Cut a card back to the right size for the combined height of the mirror and fireplace, allowing room for the mantelpiece and cornice.

7 Build up the mantelpiece with layers of card, to fit the space allowed. Spray paint the step, surround and mantel-piece assembly.

8 Fix the tiled card pieces in place and glue the fireplace to the card back.

9 Use more card to make a top, sides and shelf for the overmantel. Score vertical lines on the front of the shelf.

10 Decorate the sides with the turned banisters.

11 Glue the hairslide to the top of the overmantel. Cut the top section off the dolls' house balustrade. Glue the top section below the mantel shelf and the bottom section above it.

12 Add pillars of balsa wood to each side and top these with the decorative beads threaded onto pins, pressing the pins into the balsa.

13 Decorate the front of the pillars with the long jewellery findings, and join the pillars to the mantelpiece. Add the stick-on furniture decorations.

14 Cover the fireplace surround and mantelpiece before spray painting the overmantel, then fix the mirror in place.

For details of vases, mantel clocks, framed pictures and fireguard see Chapter 5, pages 110, 112, 113 and 114.

Arts and Crafts Movement Overmantel

The Arts and Crafts Movement simplified everything it could and if it couldn't simplify, painted the detail white! Overmantels stayed in vogue though, so here is a slightly simpler version of the Victorian Overmantel shown on page 20.

MATERIALS

Foamboard
Balsa
Black card (or plain
    card painted)
Card
Sections from dolls'
    house balustrade
Jewellery findings
Stick-on furniture
    decoration, strip
Haze air freshener pack
Mirror from a make-up
    compact
Small, curved bubble pack

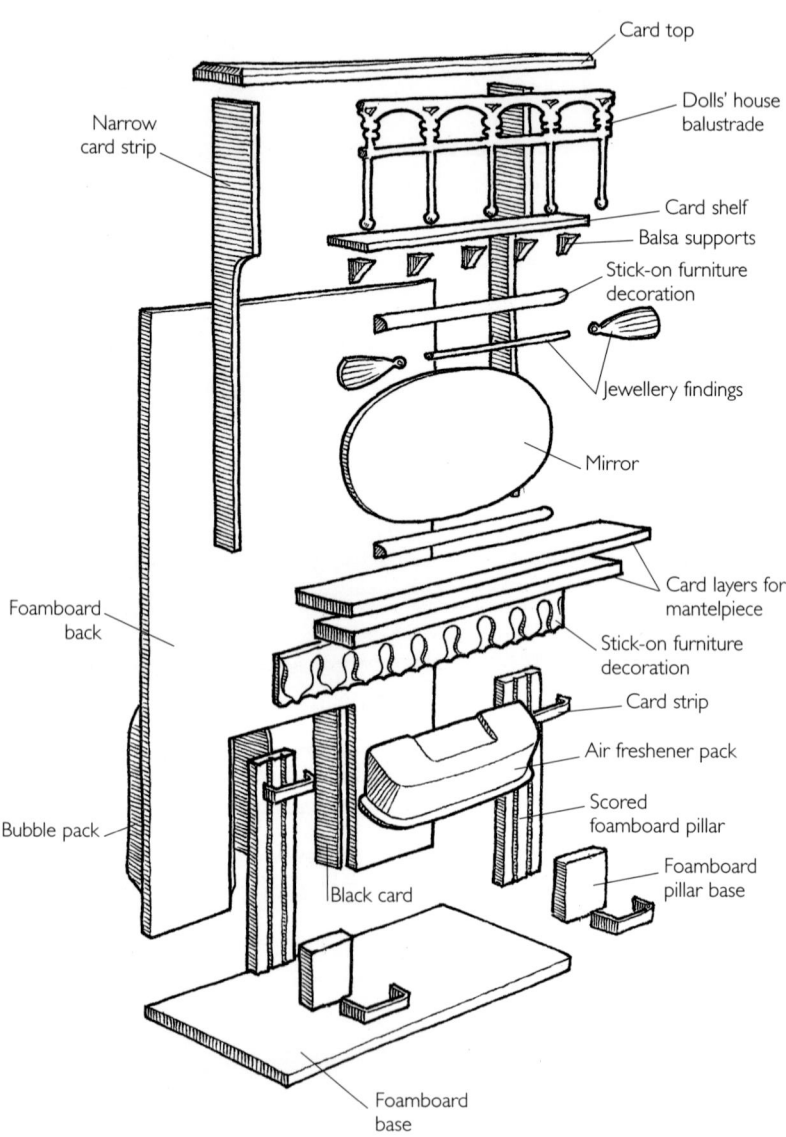

Card top

Dolls' house balustrade

Narrow card strip

Card shelf

Balsa supports

Stick-on furniture decoration

Jewellery findings

Mirror

Foamboard back

Card layers for mantelpiece

Stick-on furniture decoration

Card strip

Air freshener pack

Scored foamboard pillar

Foamboard pillar base

Bubble pack

Black card

Foamboard base

METHOD

1 Cut one piece of foamboard to the height of the fireplace and overmantel combined.

2 Cut a rectangle from this for the fireplace, adding two strips of black card at either side.

3 Cut a piece from the air freshener pack for the hood and fit it in place, then back the fireplace opening with the bubble pack.

4 Score vertical lines on a second piece of foamboard and cut two pillars from this. Flank the fireplace with these pillars, adding blocks of foamboard for the column bases and foamboard strips of card to band around the tops and bases.

5 Run a length of stick-on furniture strip above the hood and pillars for decoration.

6 Build a mantelpiece shelf from layers of card and glue into position.

7 Position the mirror and mark where it should go, but do not yet glue in place.

8 Cut and position a card top for the overmantel.

9 Cut two narrow strips of card to run vertically at each side of the mirror, from the mantelpiece to the overmantel top.

10 Add a card shelf above the mirror as attachment points so that the balustrade can stand proud. Glue the section of balustrade in place and add wedges of balsa as supports.

11 Decorate the front of the overmantel with jewellery findings and bands of stick-on furniture decoration, and spray paint the whole assembly white.

12 Fix the mirror in place, and set the fireplace on a foamboard base, covered with black card.

For details of brassware, candlesticks, mantel clock and fireguard see Chapter 5, pages 107, 111, 112 and 114.

Comfy Cosy Brick Fireplace

You can make this sort of cosy fireplace to any shape or size: this particular example is modelled on my own full-size hearth.

MATERIALS

Foamboard
Card

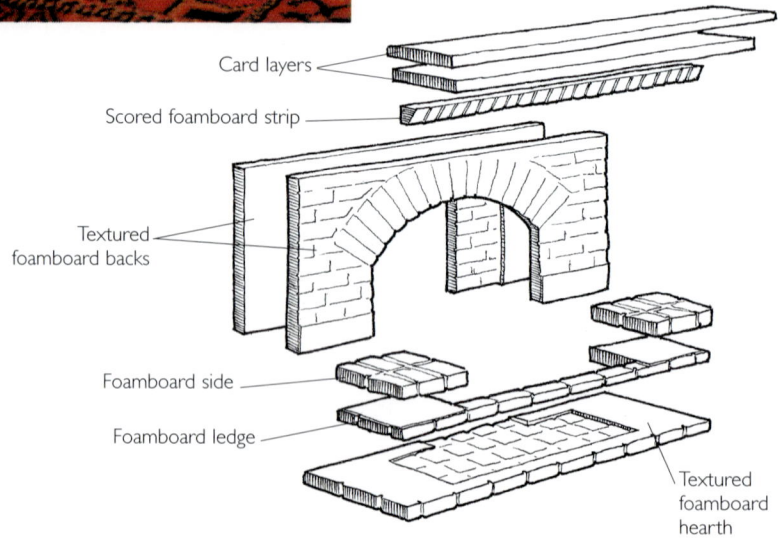

Card layers

Scored foamboard strip

Textured foamboard backs

Foamboard side

Foamboard ledge

Textured foamboard hearth

METHOD

1 Plan your fireplace by drawing it lightly on the foamboard. You will want two large pieces for the back and a smaller piece the same width as the back for the step. Strip the top layer of card from these pieces to expose the foam layer.

2 Cut a wide arch from one back piece, for the fireplace opening, a narrower arch from the second back piece, and a rectangle from the step for the hearth. Texture the backs to resemble bricks and the rectangle cut from the hearth to resemble tiles (see Brickwork, page 14).

3 Layer pieces of card to build up an overlapping mantel-piece. Spray paint before fixing in place.

4 Cut a thin strip of foamboard to set under the mantelpiece, giving it a slightly curved front. Score on brick markings and fix in place.

5 Assemble the fireplace backs and step. The back piece with the narrower arch will form the pillars inside the fireplace and should be placed behind the other piece.

6 Cut two more layers of foamboard for the fender, to build up the front ledge and two sides. Score the brick texture onto each piece.

7 Paint all the textured foam-board with watercolours.

For details of brassware, ornaments, vases and framed pictures see Chapter 5, pages 107, 108, 110 and 113.

Stockbroker Tudor Inglenook

Very easy to make, this brick fireplace gives a cosy, homely look to any dolls' house room.

MATERIALS

Foamboard
Drop earrings with
    pointed ends
Rectangular lozenge from a
    chain belt
Buckle from a chain belt
Card
Balsa wood
Small curtain ring

METHOD*

1   Cut a piece of foamboard 7⁷/₈ in (200mm) square and remove the top card layer to score brickwork lines on the foam (see Brickwork, page 14). Paint the piece with watercolours.

2   From this piece cut a back, a hearth and two sides for the fireplace. Assemble these pieces to make an open box.

3   Fix two brick 'steps' in place at either side of the fireplace and add seats made from painted card.

4   Cut and paint a balsa beam for the mantelpiece and two sides to fit inside the fireplace. (I used watercolours.)

5   For the log holder, mount the belt buckle on a base of balsa to give it height.

6   Glue the rectangular lozenge to the base of the buckle, so that it juts forwards, to form the grate.

7 Make two front legs from balsa to support the grate.

8 Cut the curtain ring in half and mount a drop earring on each half. Disguise the balsa legs with these, using the curtain ring halves as the feet.

9 Spray paint the log holder before positioning it in the inglenook.

★ FOR SETTING THE INGLENOOK SEE INSTALLING A FIREPLACE, PAGE 16.

For details of brassware, vases, candlesticks and mantel clock see Chapter 5, pages 107, 110, 111 and 112.

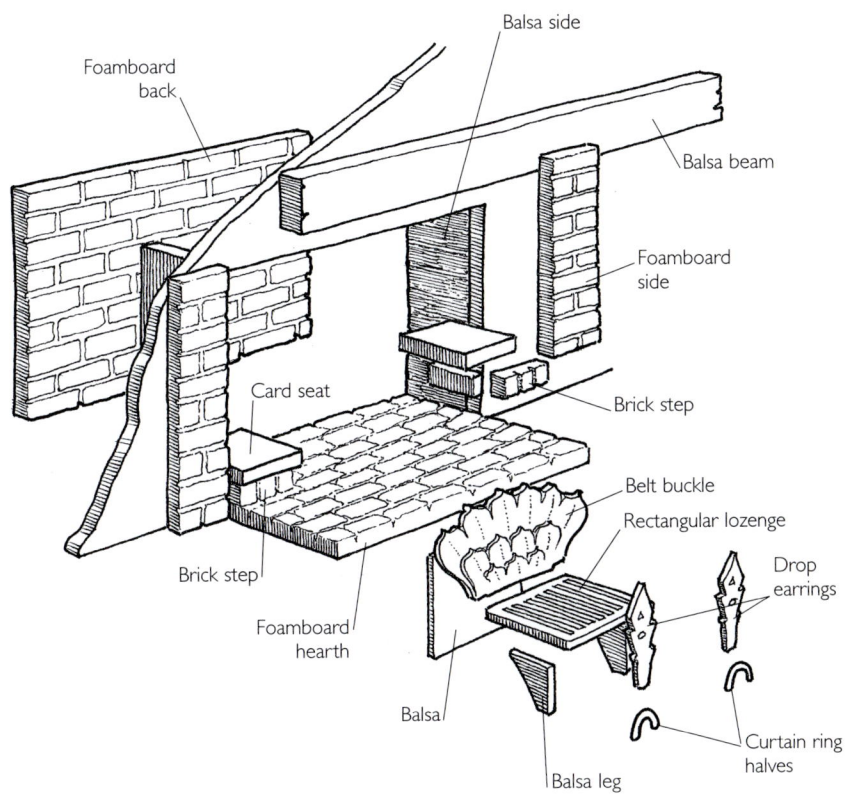

Balsa side

Foamboard back

Balsa beam

Foamboard side

Card seat

Brick step

Belt buckle

Rectangular lozenge

Drop earrings

Brick step

Foamboard hearth

Balsa

Curtain ring halves

Balsa leg

Antiques Roadshow Gotcha

There is always that moment in the *Antiques Roadshow* programmes when the expert asks, 'Do you have any idea what it is worth?', and the victim lies through their teeth. Well, this fireplace would cost you a fortune if it was slightly larger, but you can have it for next to nothing if you make it like this.

MATERIALS

Fancy picture frame,
   6 x 4in (152 x 102mm)
Black card
   (or plain card painted)
Throwaway razor blade guard
Small filigree bracelet link
Sheet of tiles, to scale
Pyramid-shaped box
   (I used the box from an
   individual portion of
   Chavroux cheese)
Lolly mould
Railway fencing, 00 gauge
Cocktail forks x 4
Stick-on furniture
   decoration, strip
Large rectangular bracelet link
Long bracelet link

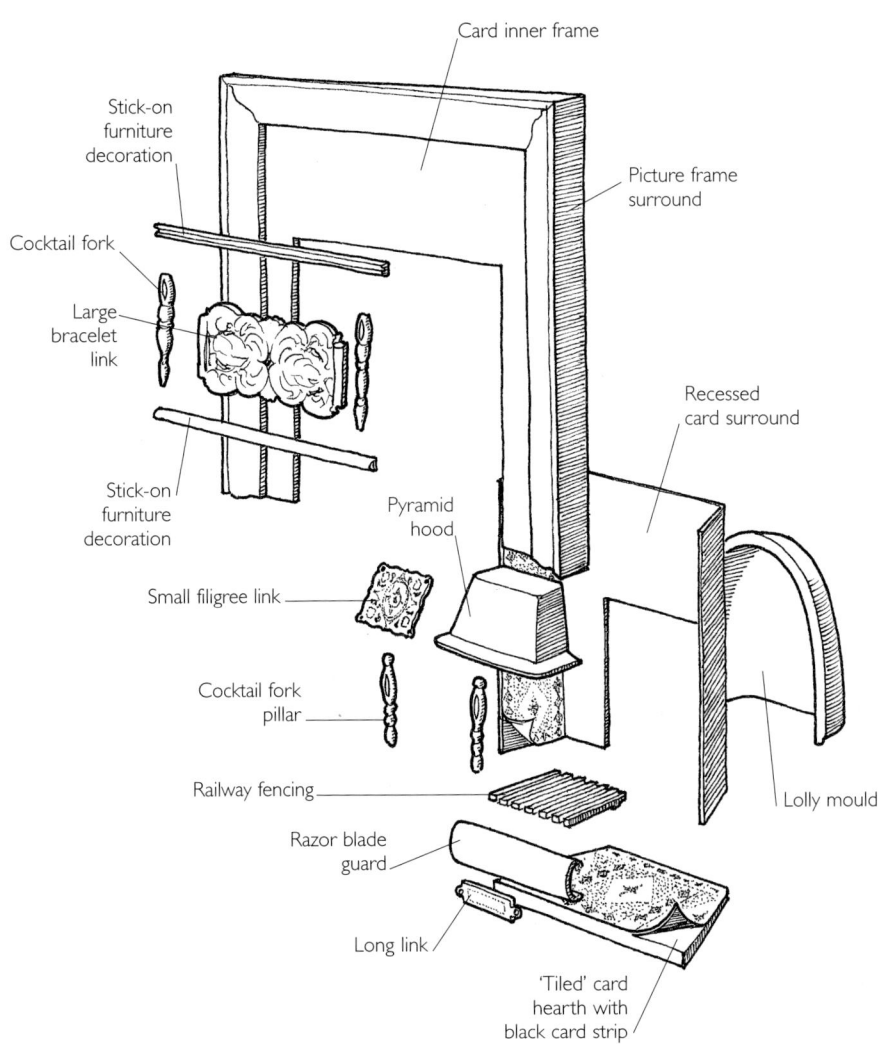

Card inner frame

Stick-on
furniture
decoration

Picture frame
surround

Cocktail fork

Large
bracelet
link

Recessed
card surround

Stick-on
furniture
decoration

Pyramid
hood

Small filigree link

Cocktail fork
pillar

Railway fencing

Lolly mould

Razor blade
guard

Long link

'Tiled' card
hearth with
black card strip

METHOD

1 Cut the bottom inch (25mm) or so off the picture frame. (The bottom piece can be used as a fender, but it was not used for this project.)

2 Cut an inner frame from the black card, making the top of the frame quite deep (see drawing).

3 Cut, score and bend more card to make a recessed fireplace surround and hearth. Cut a rectangular opening from the centre of the surround to take the grate.

4 Back the hole with a lolly mould painted black and insert a piece of railway fencing in the opening as a grate basket.

5 Front the rectangular space with the razor blade guard for a fender.

6 Cut the pyramid-shaped box in half vertically and place one half above the hole as a hood.

7 Cut two cocktail forks to size for the pillars between the hood and the guard.

8 Tile the hearth and the fireplace surround and tidy the front of the hearth with a strip of black card.

9 Decorate the top of the inner frame with strips of stick-on furniture decoration, the large bracelet link and two cocktail forks cut to fit.

10 Add the long link to the front of the fender and the small filigree link to the hood.

11 Hand paint all the parts that should be black, leaving the long link to stand out.

Tudor Cudd Open Hearth

Tudor Cudd was the illegitimate son of one of the Henrys. (I've no idea which, but as long as they knew . . .) The original fire basket that inspired all the modern copies so beloved by yuppies and stockbrokers was discovered in his remote castle somewhere on the Scottish borders. Here it is in miniature.

MATERIALS

End clasp of chain belt
Large selection of beads
String of beads
Drop earring
Earring curlicues x 1 pair
Toy farm fencing
Jewellery findings
Firm card
Balsa wood
Dressmakers' pins x 4
Child's hair comb
Bead caps x 2

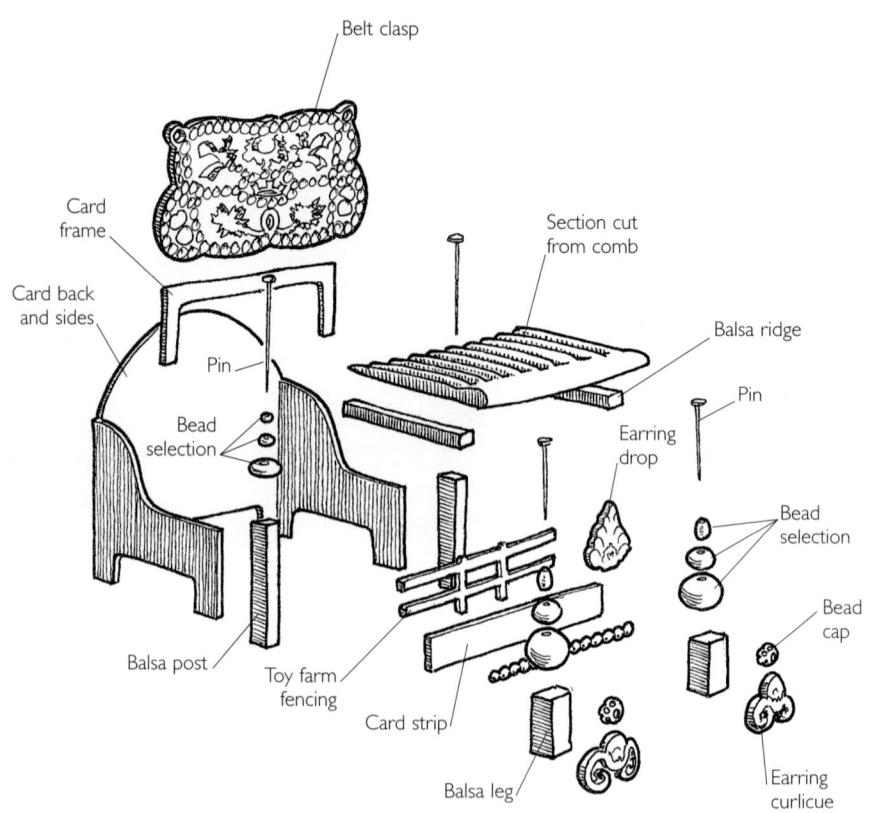

Belt clasp

Card frame

Card back and sides

Section cut from comb

Balsa ridge

Pin

Pin

Bead selection

Earring drop

Bead selection

Bead cap

Balsa post

Toy farm fencing

Card strip

Balsa leg

Earring curlicue

METHOD

1 Cut, score and bend card to form the back and sides of the hearth, as illustrated.

2 Fix a little ridge of balsa on either inner side to hold the firebasket.

3 Cut a section from the comb to fit the fireplace and glue it in place, resting on the balsa pieces, to make the grate.

4 Front this grate with firebars made from the fencing, and add a balsa post to either side.

5 Thread a selection of beads onto two pins and press these into the balsa posts.

6 Decorate a strip of card with a string of beads and neaten the front of the hearth with this.

7 Place the earring drop in the centre of the firebars.

8 Glue the belt clasp to the back of the hearth for decoration. Neaten the back with a frame of card to run below this clasp and down the sides.

9 Make two front legs from balsa strip and top these with another set of beaded pins.

10 Add an earring curlicue and a bead cap to each strip to make the decorative legs and feet.

11 To finish, spray paint the whole hearth silver.

Ann Kipanki's Bedroom Warmer

Ann Kipanki worked in Sheila Blige's infamous guest house at the turn of the century, and I am told it was important that her bedroom be kept warm. No doubt she would have said the whole thing was a frame-up – and she would have been right – about the stove if not about her reputation.

MATERIALS

Small picture frames, 1
    decorative and 1 plain
Amplex breath capsules,
    handbag pack
Small bead cap
Filigree metal bracelet
Turned cocktail sticks x 2
Sheet of tiles, to scale
Curved earrings x 2
Firm card
Jewellery finding
Flat ring

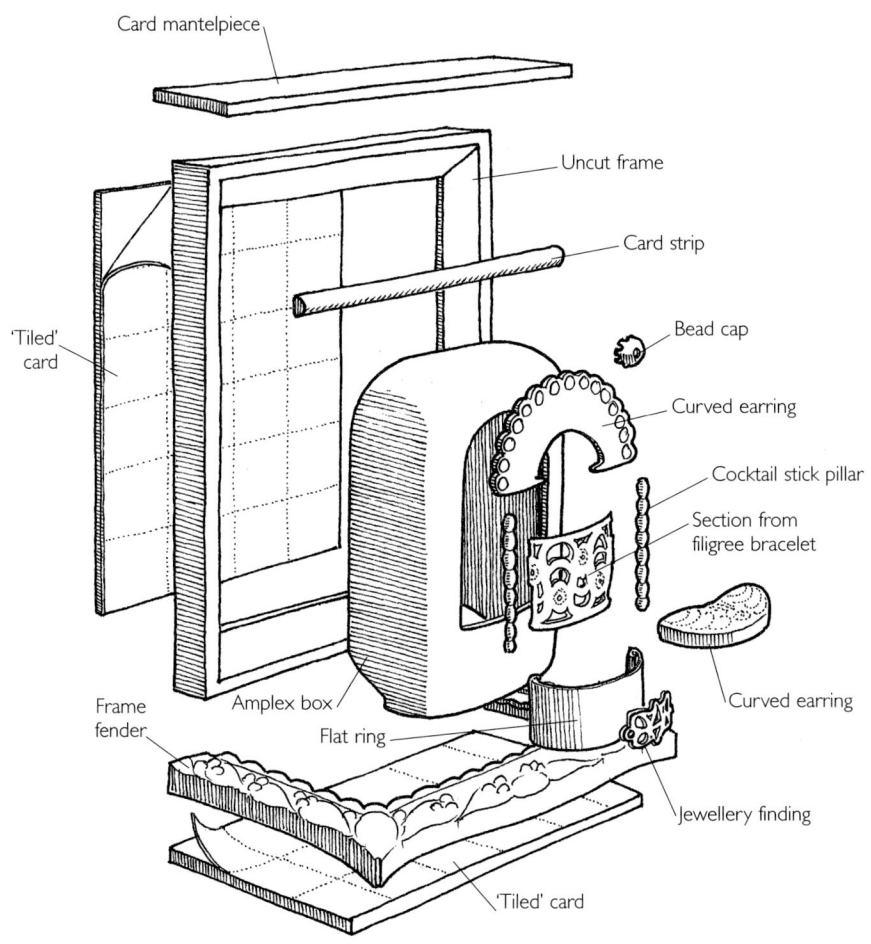

Card mantelpiece

Uncut frame

Card strip

Bead cap

'Tiled' card

Curved earring

Cocktail stick pillar

Section from filigree bracelet

Frame fender

Amplex box

Flat ring

Curved earring

Jewellery finding

'Tiled' card

METHOD

1 Cut an inch (25mm) or so off the bottom of one frame and use this for the fender. Use the other frame, uncut, for the fireplace back. Paint the base of the frame gold and the rest of the frame black.

2 Cut and tile two pieces of card to fill both the back and the hearth. Fix both card pieces in place and glue the hearth to the back.

3 Mark a horizontal line on the front of the Amplex box, $\frac{1}{2}$ in (13mm) up from the bottom. Using this line as the baseline, cut out an opening from the box. Spray paint the box black.

4 Cut a section from the filigree bracelet to fit into this opening. This forms the gas mantel. Paint it white and fix it in place.

5 Decorate the sides of the opening with turned cocktail sticks for pillars, and top it with a curved earring. Fix a bead cap above this.

6 Cut the flat ring in half. Use half the ring for the ash box, topping it with the second curved earring.

7 Cut a piece of card for the mantelpiece and cover it with the tiled sheet.

8 Add a horizontal strip of card to the fireplace back.

9 Add the jewellery finding to the base of the Amplex box as a makers' nameplate.

10 Handpaint all the gold and black parts, adding a few gold flecks to the fireplace and surround.

The Eclair Elite

What is the use of a diet if you don't break it from time to time? Personally, I dislike the itemized receipt you get from supermarkets nowadays. I was wondering how to justify the printed purchase, 'One éclair, chocolate', to the world and my own man in particular when I thought of one of my better excuses; 'The package it came in is just the right shape for a stove,' I muttered as I snuck past him. Of course, you can't use the éclair so I ate it.

MATERIALS

Eclair bubble pack
Plastic cocktail forks x 2
Stick-on furniture
    decoration, strip
Three-into-one necklace
    clasp
Jewellery findings
Balsa wood
Filigree link from chain belt
Fruit juice carton pourer
Firm card (optional)
Bracelet link

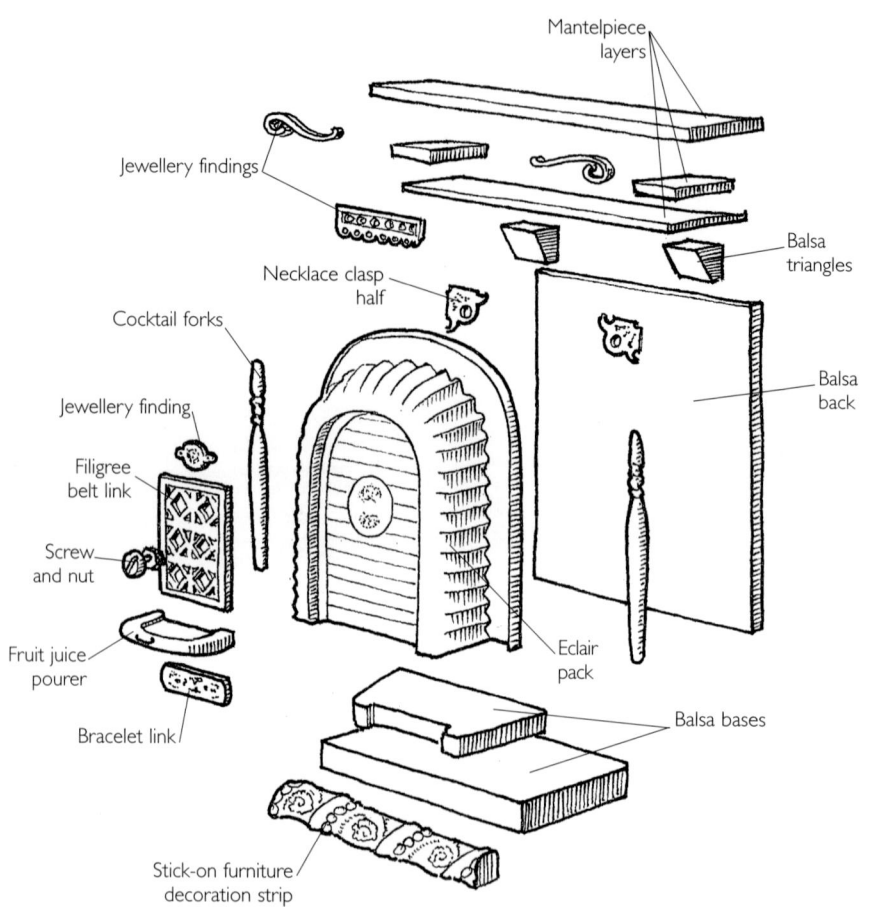

Mantelpiece layers

Jewellery findings

Balsa triangles

Necklace clasp half

Cocktail forks

Balsa back

Jewellery finding

Filigree belt link

Screw and nut

Fruit juice pourer

Eclair pack

Bracelet link

Balsa bases

Stick-on furniture decoration strip

METHOD

1 Using one side of the éclair pack, cut across the front about halfway up.

2 Cut a balsa base to fit into the open end of the horseshoe.

3 Glue this to a second base a little larger than the first.

4 Fix this whole assembly to a balsa back of $3^7/_8$ x $2^3/_4$ x $^1/_4$ in (100 x 70 x 5mm).

5 Run a length of the furniture decoration strip along the front of the balsa base to hide the cut edge.

6 Cut two cocktail forks to use as pillars on either side of the fireplace and top these with graduated triangles of balsa.

7 Cut the necklace clasp into halves to decorate the top corners, above the arch.

8 Build up the mantelpiece with layers of balsa or card as shown in the diagram.

9 Decorate the mantel with jewellery findings.

10 Use the filigree link from the chain belt as a door, fixing it centre front. Add a screw, complete with nut, for a handle. Add a jewellery finding above the door for decoration.

11 Cut the fruit juice pourer to use as a sill and glue it below the door.

12 Glue a bracelet link below the door for an ash pan door.

13 Spray paint the whole stove grey with a dusting of gold.

The Fabulous Foundation Fireplace

This is a fireplace of an altogether different complexion – and I use the word advisedly! Should you desire a lovely skin as well as a fireplace, this is the one for you. Many popular brands sell square refills of compressed powder for their compacts: the bubble packs these come in are virtually ready-made fireplaces, with all the mouldings already there. They are, I have to warn you, a trifle too big for 1/12 scale, but a fireplace made from them would look good in a child's dolls' house.

MATERIALS

Compressed powder
    refill pack
Filigree metal bracelet link
Rectangular link from
    chain belt
Jewellery findings
Card

METHOD

1 Cut, score and bend the card to make the front section attached to the refill pack.
2 Fix the rectangular belt link in the opening.
3 Cut a sill from card and attach it below the link.

4 Top the fireplace opening with a card lid and finish with the filigree bracelet link.
5 Decorate the fireplace with various jewellery findings.
6 Mask the rectangular link and spray paint black.

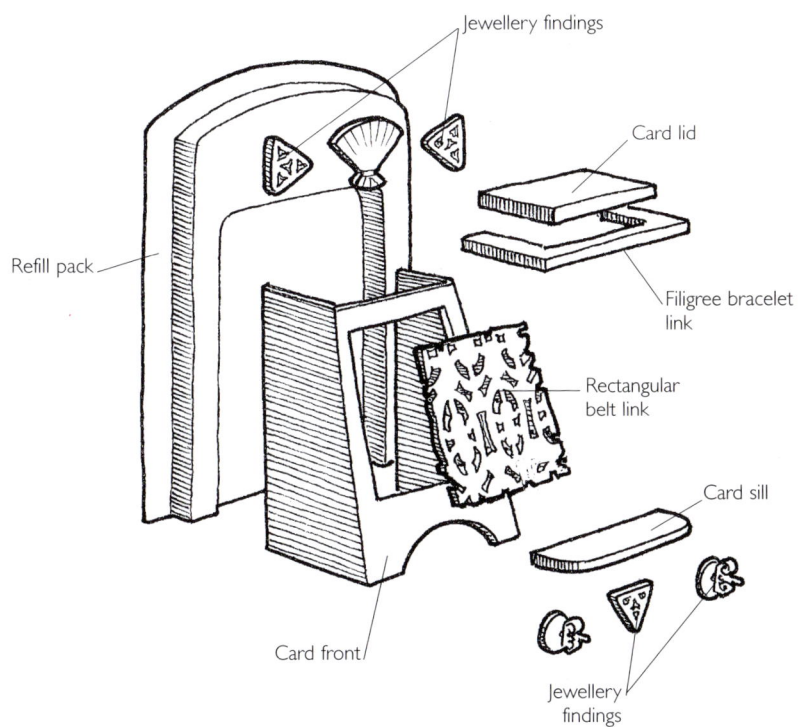

Jewellery findings

Card lid

Refill pack

Filigree bracelet link

Rectangular belt link

Card sill

Card front

Jewellery findings

Cast Iron Fireplaces

These little beauties used to be in bedrooms. We all had them stripped out, but now we are busy buying them back at hugely inflated prices and reinstalling them. However, making them for your dolls' house won't cost you a bomb and they really are easy. There are so many different things that can be used to good effect that I hope you will use my ideas only as a guide and try different combinations for yourself.

MATERIALS

Use any or all of these
Card
Kinder eggs
Sweetener packs,
    handbag size
Individual portion butter tubs
Individual portion cream tubs
Plastic doily sections
Jewellery findings
Bangle links
Belt links
Balsa wood
Cocktail sticks
Cocktail forks
Plastic tea stirrers
Beads

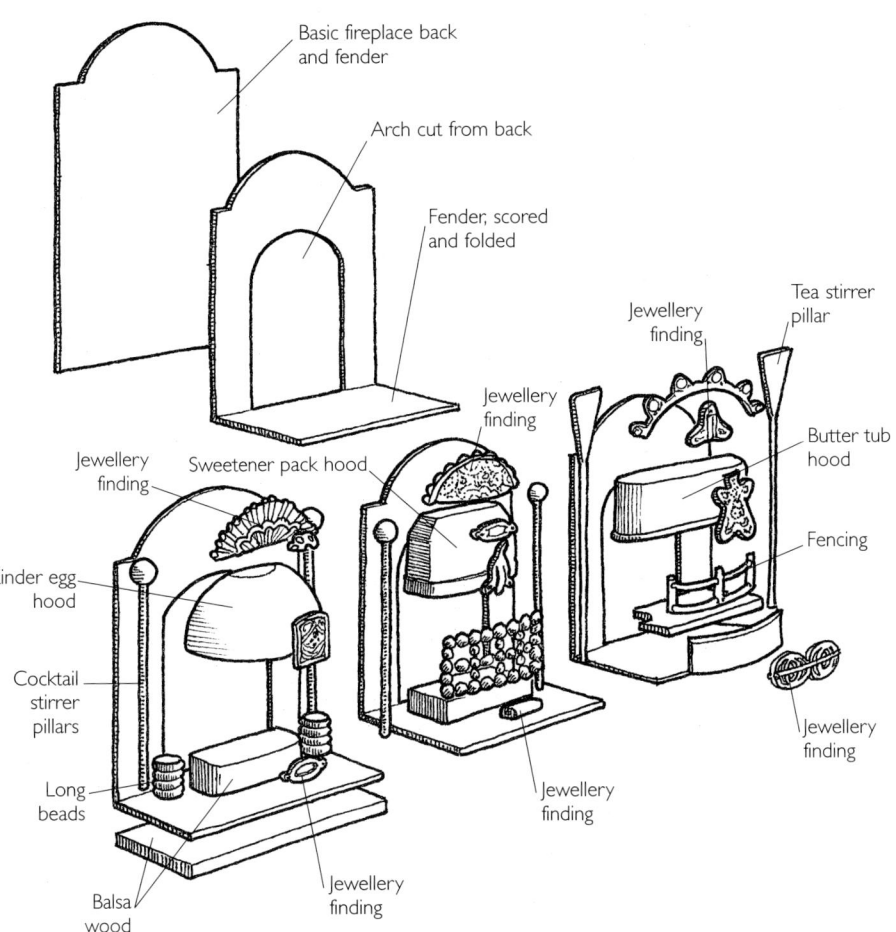

Basic fireplace back and fender

Arch cut from back

Fender, scored and folded

Tea stirrer pillar

Jewellery finding

Jewellery finding

Butter tub hood

Jewellery finding

Sweetener pack hood

Fencing

Jewellery finding

Kinder egg hood

Cocktail stirrer pillars

Jewellery finding

Long beads

Jewellery finding

Balsa wood

Jewellery finding

METHOD

1 Cut the basic shape of the fireplace back and fender from card.
2 Score and bend the fender and cut out an arch from the centre of the back.
3 For the hood, use a section from a Kinder egg, butter tub or sweetener pack.
4 For the base, cut another section from any of the above or from balsa.
5 Flank the fireplace with pillars made from such things as turned cocktail sticks, cocktail forks or tea stirrers.
6 Decorate the hood with jewellery findings or sections cut from a doily.
7 Add a link or similar to the base as a makers' nameplate.
8 The uniting factor is to spray paint the whole caboodle black (see photo), though odd findings can be added as shiny decorations or gas mantels.

CHAPTER 3
COOKING STOVES

1920s Fish and Chip Shop

When Hal Ebbut wed Anne Chovey their dream was to have a plaice of their own. They opened up their fish and chip shop in the 1920s, with a coal-fired oven, massive chip fryer and, in pride of place and full view of the customers, a state of the art chip cutter.

MATERIALS

OVEN AND CHIP SCOOP
Foamboard
Firm card
Black card (or plain
    card painted)
Embossed links from a
    chain belt x 2
Long chain links x 7
Stick-on furniture decorations
Oval links x 2
Sheet of tiles, to scale
Turned banister rod
Mirror from a
    powder compact
Brass shim
Individual portion pickle tub
Brass button, with a shaft
Christmas tree light shade
Tiny brass bell
Brass wire
Brass washer
Brooch
Jewellery findings x 2

MATERIALS

COUNTER
Card
Foamboard
Small buttons or beads
Sheet of tiles, to scale

CUTTER
Turned cocktail stick
Balsa
Embossed metal earring
Tiny square frame
Small section of mesh

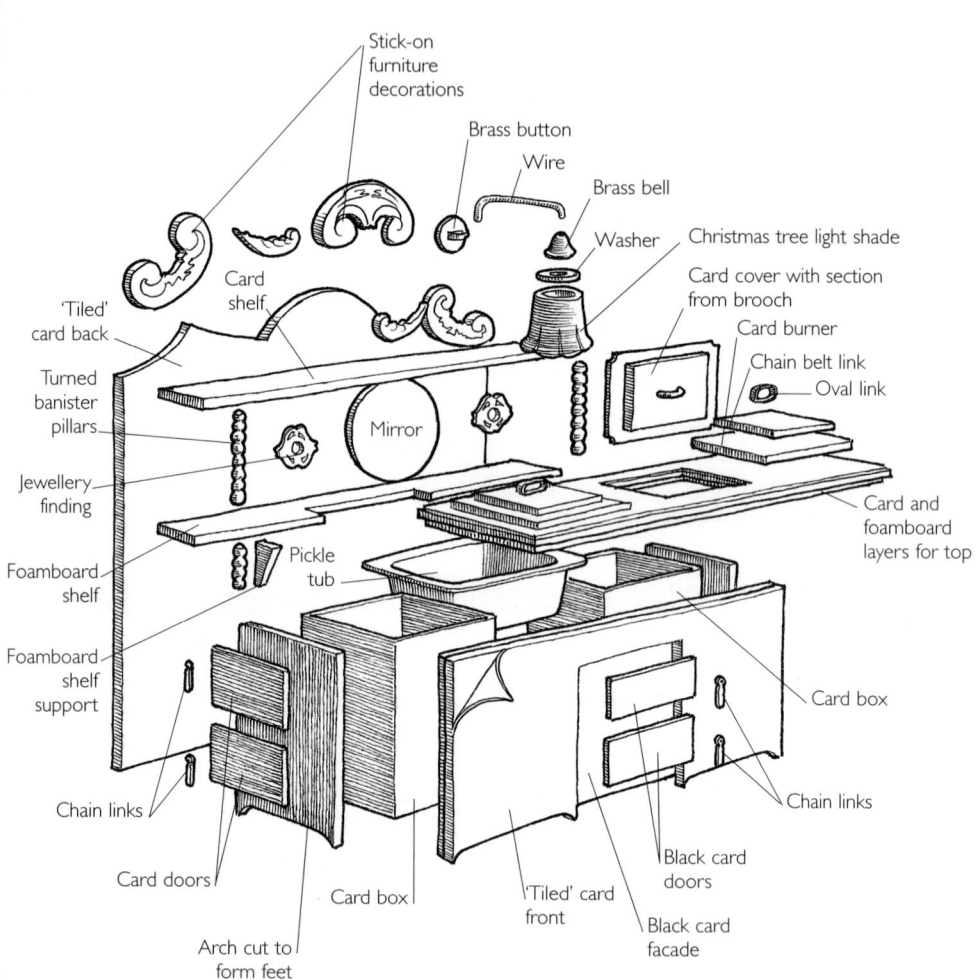

Stick-on furniture decorations

Brass button

Wire

Brass bell

Washer

Christmas tree light shade

Card cover with section from brooch

Card shelf

Card burner

'Tiled' card back

Chain belt link

Oval link

Turned banister pillars

Mirror

Jewellery finding

Card and foamboard layers for top

Foamboard shelf

Pickle tub

Foamboard shelf support

Card box

Chain links

Chain links

Card doors

Black card doors

Card box

'Tiled' card front

Arch cut to form feet

Black card facade

METHOD

OVEN AND CHIP SCOOP

1 Make or find two card boxes, $2^3/8$ x $1^5/8$ in (60 x 40mm), and space them on a sheet of card, allowing room between them for the pickle tub.

2 Draw around these assembled parts onto the card. This will establish the rough size of the oven base.

3 Cut out the base following this outline, then cut another piece of card to the same width, for the back. Cut this back piece so that it extends above the two boxes.

4 Lay furniture decorations across the top of the back and decide the shape accordingly. Mark the shape on, remove the decorations, and cut the card following this outline.

5 Glue the two boxes and the back in place on the base. For extra detail, cut out arches from their fronts and sides to form feet.

6 Paint the pickle tub silver and place it between the boxes.

7 Cover the boxes and pickle tub with a black card facade, then add an extra card front, with a rectangle cut from the centre. Tile this extra front and fix in place.

8 Cut two black card doors to fix to the black card in this rectangular opening. Use chain links for the door handles.

9 Tile the stove back and add two card doors apiece to the box sides. Again, use chain links for door handles.

10 Cut a piece of foamboard to run across the top of this assembly, with a rectangle cut from the centre, where the chip fryer will be located.

11 Cut two overhanging tops from card, one slightly smaller than the other, both with a rectangular opening cut from the centre.

12 Glue all three pieces in place, foamboard first, then larger top followed by smaller top.

13 Add a card burner topped by a chain belt link and an oval link at either side.

14 Arrange and stick the furniture decorations in place.

15 Position the mirror on the stove back. Cut a foamboard shelf and supports to run across the back below this. Remove a section from the centre of the shelf to accommodate the chip fryer lid.

16 Paint two jewellery findings white and fix in place on either side of the mirror.

17 Cut a smaller card shelf to run just below the decorated top. Fix the top shelf in place, then cut pillars from the turned banister and position on either side of the back, below each shelf.

18 Tile the bottom shelf then fix it and its supports in place.

19 Make a card cover for the chip fryer and top this with a section cut from a brooch for the handle.

20 For the light, glue the bell to the washer and top the Christmas tree light shade with this ensemble.

21 Bend the wire to form an 'S' shape, and thread one end into the bell top.

22 Glue the front of the button onto the back wall and thread the other end of the wire through its shaft.

23 Paint the base of the button and all the exposed areas of card cream.

24 Cut, score and bend the shim to form the chip scoop, adding a long chain link for the handle.

COUNTER

1 Make a card box about the same length as the oven.

2 Cut a top and a base for the box from foamboard and fix these in place.

3 Add an overhanging card counter to the top.

4 Add a card back – higher than the counter to keep the ravening hordes at bay.

5 Score the back to look like planking (see photo on page 47) and add a thin card strip along the base.

6 To the other side of the counter add false card doors with buttons or beads for handles. Add a card panel to either side of the counter.

7 Tile the 'splashback' and top it with a tiled shelf. Add card shelf supports to either side.

8 Paint the cupboards and the back of the counter green and, while the paint is still wet, drag your brush over to show the underlying white of the card in a grain pattern.

9 Paint the counter top and a strip along the base of the splashback black, then paint the shelf supports black.

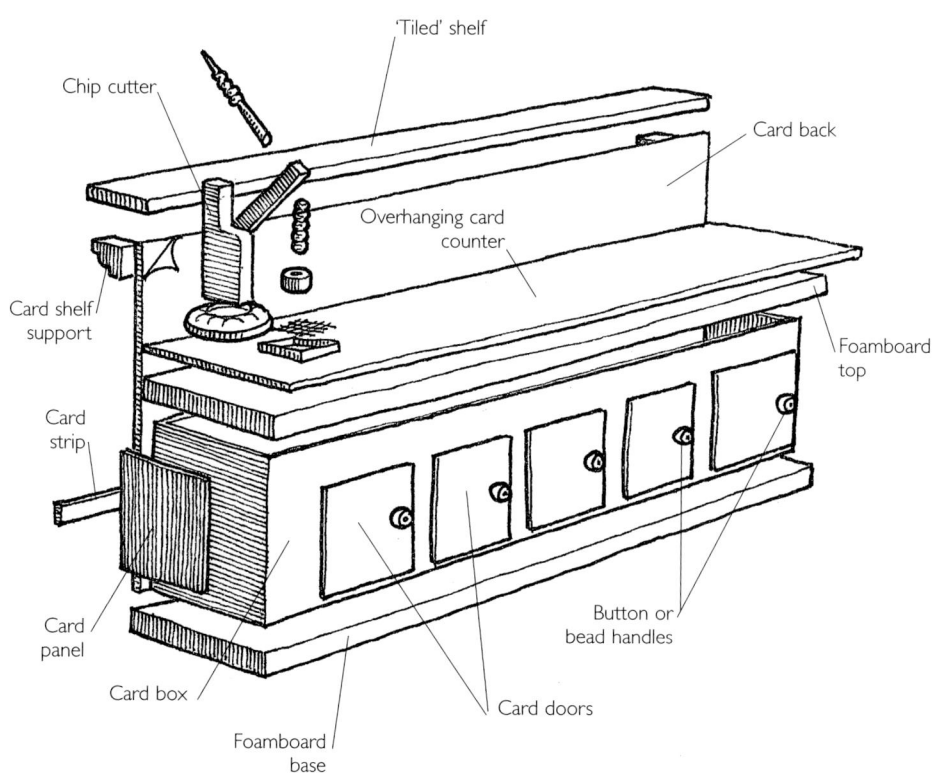

'Tiled' shelf

Chip cutter

Card back

Overhanging card counter

Card shelf support

Foamboard top

Card strip

Card panel

Button or bead handles

Card box

Card doors

Foamboard base

10 Finally, add a coat of varnish to any parts where a shine is required.

CUTTER

1 The main frame of the cutter is made from a turned cocktail stick and balsa, as illustrated.

2 Mount this assembly on an embossed metal earring.

3 If you can find a tiny square frame, cut a piece of mesh to fit inside and glue in place.

4 Fix this on the counter in front of the main frame.

For details of brassware, ornaments, pots and pans (including chip scoop) and bottles see Chapter 5, pages 107, 108 and 109.

The Megalith Kitchen Range

Ella Mentry the cook was unusually polite to her orphan helper and referred to her as 'my dear Watson'. Watson's job was to keep the kitchen range clean and stoked while Ella's was to produce a variety of excellent meals for Major Rhodeahead and the Mem Saab.

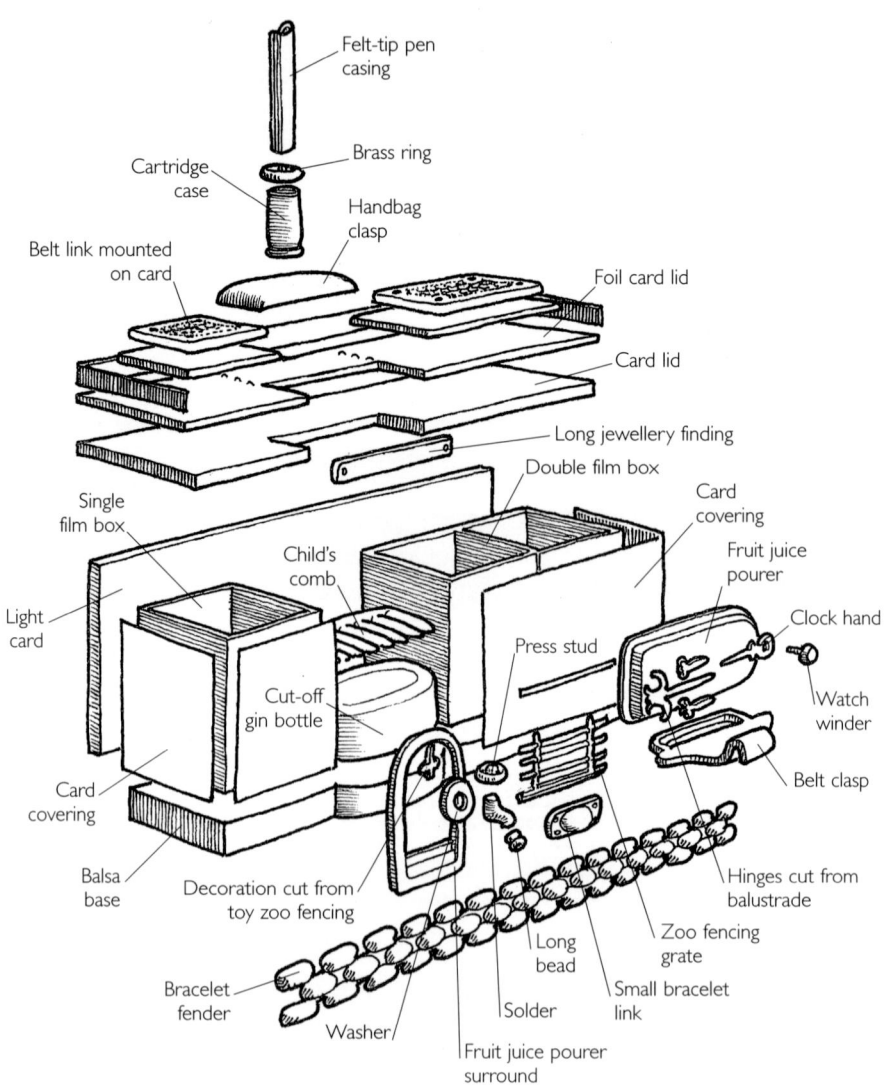

Felt-tip pen casing

Brass ring

Cartridge case

Handbag clasp

Belt link mounted on card

Foil card lid

Card lid

Long jewellery finding

Double film box

Single film box

Card covering

Child's comb

Fruit juice pourer

Light card

Clock hand

Press stud

Cut-off gin bottle

Watch winder

Card covering

Belt clasp

Balsa base

Decoration cut from toy zoo fencing

Hinges cut from balustrade

Zoo fencing grate

Long bead

Bracelet fender

Small bracelet link

Washer

Solder

Fruit juice pourer surround

MATERIALS

35mm film boxes x 3
Fruit juice carton pourers x 2
Plastic dolls' house balustrade
Links from metal
    chain belt x 2
Plastic gin bottle miniature
Clasp from metal chain belt
Child's curved hair comb
Balsa wood
Watch winder or bead
Brass cartridge
Foil card
    (from takeaway boxes)
Light card

Firm card
Toy zoo fencing
Handbag clasp
Small bracelet link
Long bead
Solder strip
Press stud
Felt-tip pen
Clock hand
Jewellery findings
Washer
Small brass ring
Solid chain link bracelet

METHOD*

1 Cut the bottom half inch (25mm) off the gin bottle and turn it upside down.
2 Glue two film boxes together side by side.
3 Place the cut-off bottle, the single box and the double box in a row, and back them with a piece of light card. This forms the basis of the stove.
4 Cover the boxes with card pieces cut to fit.
5 Cut a balsa base to fit: this will keep the assembly firm.
6 For the ash basket, cut the child's comb to fit, and for the firebars, cut the zoo fencing to fit in front of the bottle. Fix both in place.
7 Turn the oven upside down and trace around it onto firm card. Use this outline to make a card lid, recessing it to accommodate the fire. Fix the lid in place.
8 Using the same template, make a second lid from foil card, adding a little extra all around to allow for narrow splashbacks.

9 Use a compass point to impress rivets from the card side of the foil card, then glue this second lid, foil side up, on top of the first.

10 Stick a metal belt link, mounted on card, on each side for the cooking plates, and glue the handbag clasp in the centre to take the chimney. Mount the cartridge case in the centre of the handbag clasp.

11 Attach one of the fruit juice carton pourers to the wider side as an oven door and add fancy hinges made from decorative sections cut from dolls' house balustrade.

12 Use the clock hand, with a watch winder, for an interesting door handle.

13 Cut a slit just under this door and insert the belt clasp to form a shelf.

14 Take the lid off the other fruit juice carton pourer and use the surround as a frame. Fix it vertically on the side of the single film box.

15 Now you need a tap. Mount the washer in the centre of the frame you have just made, then bend a length of solder strip into an 'S' shape and stick it to the washer. Add a press stud for the tap handle and a long bead for the spout. Add a decorative piece cut from toy zoo fencing above the washer.

16 Attach a small bracelet link below the grate for the makers' nameplate.

17 Finish the recessed top of the firebox by neatening with a long jewellery finding.

18 Spray paint the whole assembly and leave to dry.

19 Thread the casing from the felt-tip pen through the brass ring, and attach it to the cartridge case.

20 Position the bracelet around the base for a fender.

★ FOR SETTING THE RANGE SEE INSTALLING A FIREPLACE, PAGE 16.

For details of brassware, ornaments and vases see Chapter 5, pages 107, 108 and 110.

MATERIALS

Box, 4 x 2 x 3½ in
   (102 x 51 x 89mm)
   (or firm card to make
   a box)
Flip-top lids from shampoo
   or lotion bottles x 2
Firm card
Light card
Brass tube or wire
Black paper
Oval chain link
Tiny dome shapes x 3
   (I used plastic animal eyes)
Mouldings from clear plastic
   display trays
Balsa wood
Cored solder
Split pins x 2
Brass beads x 2
Cartridge case
Brass washer
Black felt-tip pen
Watch winders x 2
Silver sequins x 2
Hairpins x 5
Pierced earring butterfly

Iwanna
AGA Cooker

As I soaked in the bath I caught sight of the plastic containers on the shelf. 'Eureka,' I yelled, 'that's what I need for the AGA plates!' I lost no time rushing to the chemist to purchase two matching containers of baby oil with white tops – maybe I should have got dressed first!

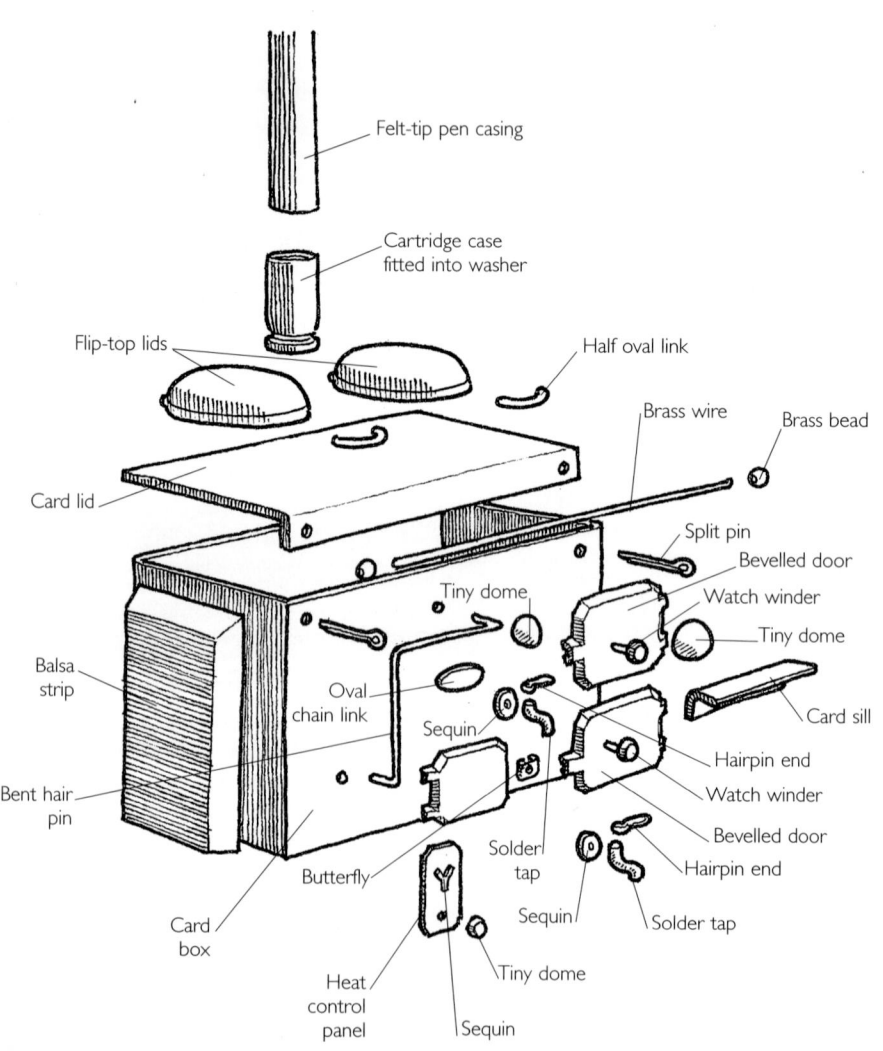

Felt-tip pen casing

Cartridge case
fitted into washer

Flip-top lids

Half oval link

Brass wire

Brass bead

Card lid

Split pin

Bevelled door

Watch winder

Tiny dome

Tiny dome

Balsa
strip

Oval
chain link

Card sill

Sequin

Hairpin end

Bent hair
pin

Watch winder

Bevelled door

Hairpin end

Butterfly

Solder
tap

Sequin

Solder tap

Card
box

Heat
control
panel

Tiny dome

Sequin

METHOD

1 Examine the bases of the clear trays in supermarkets: they often have recessed mouldings to collect any juice that runs off the produce, and this is what you are looking for. Cut these square shapes from the tray to make the distinctive bevelled doors on the AGA, using any handy bumps around the mouldings for door catches. Should these mouldings have only three sides, insert pieces of balsa into the open end as bevelled hinges. Don't use balsa for the doors – it's too grainy and will never give the characteristic shiny finish of an AGA.

2 Cover the existing box with light card, scored to bend at the corners, or make up a box from firm card.

3 Add a wide strip of balsa to the left side of the box.

4 Cut a lid from firm card, allowing a ¼ in (5mm) overlap at the front. Score along this card, ¼ in (5mm) from the front, and bend the overlap down.

5 Glue the lid to the top of the box, with the front bent down, and cover the whole top with black paper to cover the score line.

6 Remove the flip-top lids from their containers, and fix them to the top of the cooker.

7 Cut an oval link in half lengthways and glue one half to each lid for handles.

8 Fit the cartridge case into the washer and glue in place to take the downpipe (the casing from a black felt-tip pen).

9 Glue the doors in place and add one of the tiny dome shapes to the centre of the upper door.

10 To make the sill under the top door, cut a piece from light card, score and bend, then fix in place.

11 Bend a hairpin to run from the heat control panel to the top of the AGA, as shown on the illustration. Drill two holes to take the hairpin ends and disguise the top of the hairpin with a tiny dome.

12 Cut a heat control panel from card and add this to the bottom of the hairpin.

13 Add another tiny dome to the control panel, and the curved end of a hairpin as a handle. Ink on temperature

markers across the top.

14 Hand paint all the white parts of the AGA model.

15 Fix the oval chain link on the stove front, paint it with white correction fluid and ink in the letters 'AGA'.

16 Drill two holes in the lid front to take split pins and cut a length of brass wire to run between them. This will form the guard rail.

17 Attach a brass bead to either end of the guard rail.

18 Bend two small lengths of solder to form tap shapes and add handles made from the curved ends of hairpins squeezed to shape. Mount each tap on a sequin and glue them in place.

19 Finally, add watch winder handles to the doors on the right, and an earring butterfly to the door on the left.

Sears Vellot

These magnificent beasts advertised themselves as 'reverberatory ovens'. And they were, I'm told, available from Sears Roebuck by mail order! Heaven help the postman!

MATERIALS

Firm card
Rectangular chain
   belt lozenge
Filigree chain belt
   lozenges x 6
Rectangular filigree buckle
Brass wire
Tiny split pins x 6
Foil card
   (from takeaway boxes)
Balsa wood
Circular brooch finding
Stud earrings,
   including butterflies x 4
Jewellery finding
Bead caps x 4

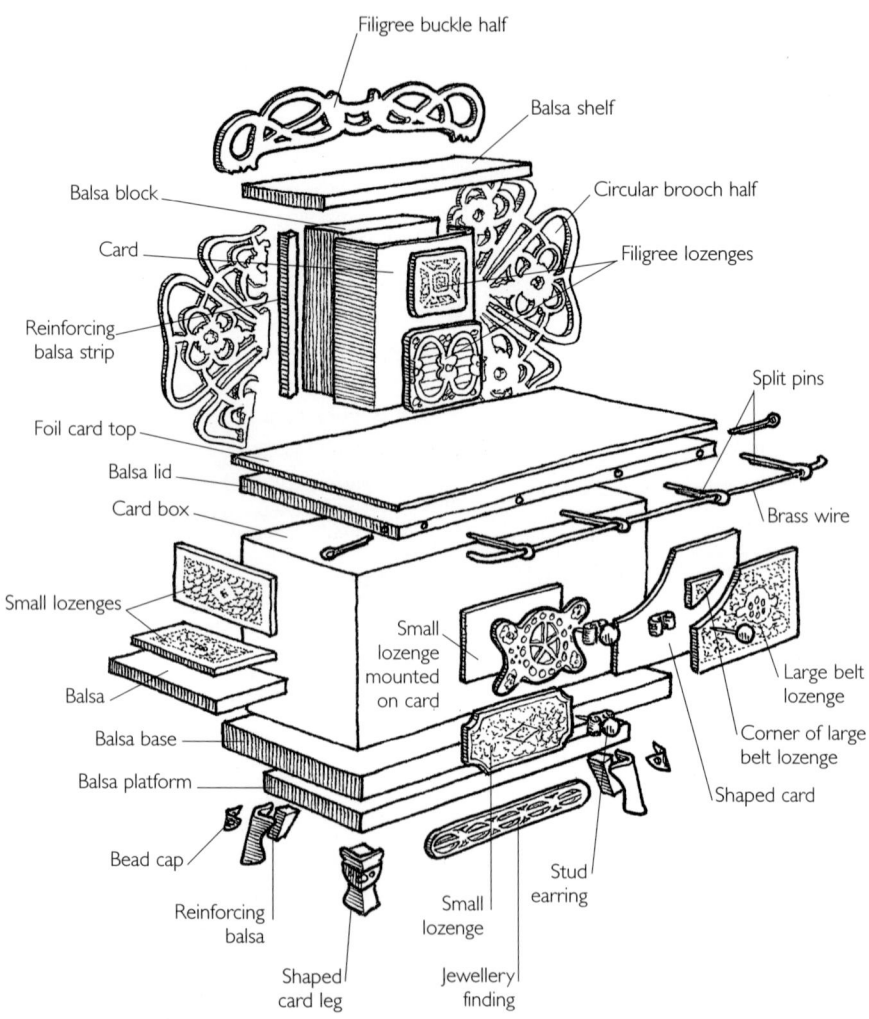

Filigree buckle half

Balsa shelf

Balsa block

Circular brooch half

Card

Filigree lozenges

Reinforcing balsa strip

Split pins

Foil card top

Balsa lid

Card box

Brass wire

Small lozenges

Small lozenge mounted on card

Large belt lozenge

Balsa

Balsa base

Corner of large belt lozenge

Balsa platform

Shaped card

Bead cap

Stud earring

Reinforcing balsa

Small lozenge

Shaped card leg

Jewellery finding

METHOD

1 Score and bend the card to make a basic box, including a top and bottom, 3½ x 1½ x 1½ in (90 x 38 x 38mm).

2 Add a balsa wood base which protrudes slightly all around.

3 Add a smaller platform below this to take the legs.

4 Cut a balsa stove lid, with an overhang on one side, and top this with a layer of foil card to give it a shiny finish.

5 Drill six holes in the balsa lid to take the guard rail.

6 Insert split pins in these holes and thread wire through them to frame the front of the stove.

7 For the chimney, wrap some card around a block of balsa and add a top shelf.

8 Cut the filigree buckle in half and use one half to frame the chimney top.

9 Cut the circular brooch in two and attach one half to each side of the chimney.

10 Reinforce this brooch decoration with a little strip of balsa on either side of the chimney.

11 Decorate the chimney front with two filigree lozenges.

12 For the distinctively shaped oven door, cut a corner off a large belt lozenge. Mount the larger section on a similarly shaped piece of card, and glue the whole in place as the door. Complete the rectangular shape by gluing the corner section in place above the oven front.

13 Add two smaller lozenges to the oven front for further doors (the top one mounted on card), and fix a final small lozenge at the top of the left side (not shown in photo).

14 Mount the last lozenge on balsa and add it to the left side as a shelf under the door.

15 Fix the earrings and butter-flies in place as door handles.

16 Cut the legs from card, then bend, curl and glue them in place so that the tops of the legs curve around the corners of the 'under base'. Bend them to look like grandma's knees, then reinforce them with balsa.

17 Decorate the front of the base with a jewellery finding and decorate the legs with bead caps.

18 Spray paint the whole stove grey and add a sprinkling of silver.

The Valor-Perfection Oil Stove

You only have to look at the Valor stove, advertised with pride in *Good Housekeeping* in 1934 as 'Perfection cooking without the fatigue of old-time methods' to see that oven design has all been downhill since then. 'Easy to clean, you can even stand it where the light is best!' And all this for 29/6: irresistible eh? Now you too can have one, and place it in the light if it so pleases you, in miniature anyway.

MATERIALS

Firm card
Tiny bottles, about
    1½in (38mm) high x 4
Drinking straw
Tiny brass beads x 2
Eye dropper lid
Button (to fit eye dropper lid)
Round chain link
Tiny chain links x 4
Clear plastic
Split pins x 2
Balsa strip
Brass washers x 4
Rectangular brass buckle
Foil card
    (from takeaway boxes)
Brass rod
Watch winder
Solder
Flattened brass ring
Brass curtain rings x 2

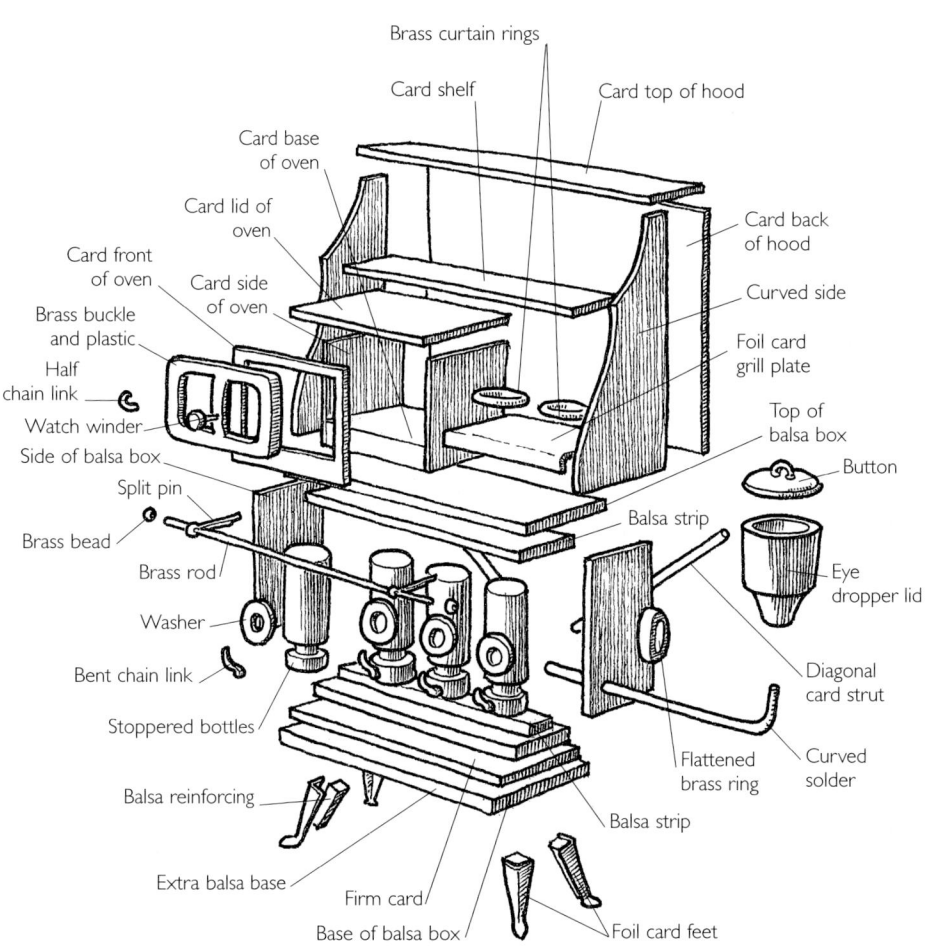

Brass curtain rings

Card shelf

Card top of hood

Card base
of oven

Card lid of
oven

Card front
of oven

Card side
of oven

Brass buckle
and plastic

Half
chain link

Watch winder

Side of balsa box

Split pin

Brass bead

Brass rod

Washer

Bent chain link

Stoppered bottles

Balsa reinforcing

Extra balsa base

Firm card

Base of balsa box

Card back
of hood

Curved side

Foil card
grill plate

Top of
balsa box

Button

Balsa strip

Eye
dropper lid

Diagonal
card strut

Curved
solder

Flattened
brass ring

Balsa strip

Foil card feet

METHOD

1 Put a small piece of drinking straw in each bottle mouth. Turn the bottles upside down.
2 Slightly bend the washers to fit the bottles' curves and fix them near the tops of the bottles, as windows.
3 Bend the tiny chain links to shape and glue to the bottle lips as gas burner handles.
4 Place all four bottles, mouths down, on a length of balsa strip cut to fit.
5 Cut a second balsa strip to the same size, and glue this to the bottle tops.
6 Glue this whole assembly to a piece of firm card cut to the same length, but slightly wider. Reinforce with balsa where necessary.
7 Make a box from balsa, with an open front and back, to enclose this. Reinforce the back of the box with two diagonal struts cut from card.
8 Add an extra layer of balsa to take the feet, but do not make the feet yet.
9 Cut the front and two sides of the oven from firm card.
10 Glue the brass buckle to the clear plastic, trimming the plastic as required, then cut a

hole from the oven box to take this ensemble. This forms the oven door.
11 Cut a chain link in half and use half for the oven door hinge. Use the watch winder for the door handle.
12 Cut a firm card base and an overlapping lid for the oven and glue in place.
13 Cut a back from card for the oven hood, and two tastefully curving sides. Cut the top curve to take a shelf, underneath which the oven will fit. Assemble the oven and hood, then cut and position the shelf and hood top, and tile the lower back.
14 Use a piece of foil card for the grill plate. Cut, score and fold over a lip at the front to make a shiny rim. Use brass curtain rings for the two grill plates.
15 Drill the two holes to take the split pins, and thread the brass rod through them for the guard rail. Finish the rod with a brass bead at each end.
16 Find a button to fit the eye dropper lid and glue it on top of the eye dropper.
17 Attach the flattened brass ring to the side of the oven, and fix

the button and eye dropper
lid to this.

18 Curve a length of solder to
make the pipe leading to the
bottles. Drill a hole in the
right-hand side of the oven to
take this, and fix the pipe in
position.

19 Cut the four feet from foil
card. Score each foot in the
centre from top to bottom
and bend along this line.

20 Curl each foot gently
outwards at the base, then
reinforce each with a strip of
balsa in the bend, at the back.

21 Paint the frame a light blue,
then mottle this with white
and darker blue.

22 When the paint is dry add a
coat of varnish.

23 Pick out the bottles and the
oil cylinder in black.

*For details of pots and pans
see Chapter 5, page 109.*

Gillette Oven

I am more or less clean-shaven myself, but nevertheless, I keep a close eye on shaving products because they provide such nice shapes for the dolls' house furnisher: an old-fashioned razor forms the basis of an upright vacuum cleaner and a six-pack of blades makes a wonderful 'stone' sink. Gillette have excelled themselves with their new safety razors. The package for the five-pack of blades is destined to make a gas oven top, as any dolls' house enthusiast will instantly recognize!

MATERIALS

Packaging from safety razor
    blade five-pack
35mm film box
Zip puller
Jewellery curlicues x 2
Butterflies from earrings x 4
Decorative jewellery
    findings x 2
Watch winders x 2
Toy zoo railing
Square watch case
Firm card
Brass tie pin
Stripwood
Black card (or plain card
    painted black)
Scrabble tile
Metal hair clip

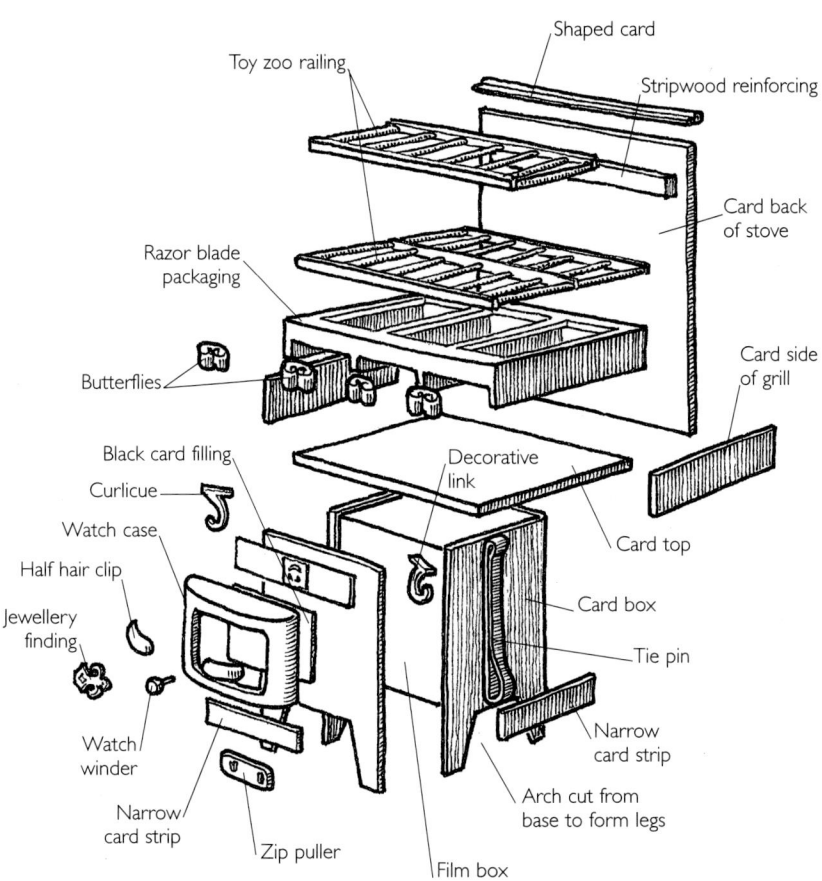

Shaped card

Toy zoo railing

Stripwood reinforcing

Card back
of stove

Razor blade
packaging

Butterflies

Card side
of grill

Black card filling

Decorative
link

Curlicue

Card top

Watch case

Half hair clip

Card box

Jewellery
finding

Tie pin

Watch
winder

Narrow
card strip

Narrow
card strip

Arch cut from
base to form legs

Zip puller

Film box

METHOD

1 Place the film box on the card and trace around it to make another, taller box. Cut, score and bend the box to enclose the film box.

2 Cut arches from the base to form legs.

3 Bind around the top and bottom of the box with a narrow strip of card, for moulding.

4 Fill in the watch case with black card to form the door, and glue this to the centre front of the box.

5 Cut the hair clip in two and stick one half on either side of the door to make a hinge and a door catch. Add a decorative finding next to one half for a hinge detail, and a watch winder to the other half for a handle.

6 Add the zip puller to the oven front, below the lower moulding, for a makers' nameplate.

7 Fix a decorative link to the centre of the upper moulding and a curlicue at either side to support the grill.

8 Cut one razor blade holder off the five-pack (it's now a four-pack), turn it upside down, and top it with a section of railing cut to fit. Set aside.

9 Cut a piece of card to the same size as your four-pack and mount it on top of the oven (so that it is supported by the curlicues).

10 Cut a card back for the stove. Attach the blade holder a little way up, then add card sides for the grill.

11 Cut a second section of railing for a plate rack and reinforce it with stripwood.

12 Run a shaped length of card across the top of the oven back to finish it off.

13 Glue the tie pin to one side of the oven, just behind the curlicue.

14 Add the four butterflies as gas taps along the front of the grill.

15 Fix a watch winder to the scrabble tile for a grill tray, as shown in the photo.

16 Paint the stove a glossy black, leaving the inside of the grill white and the brass parts as they are.

***For details of pan see
Chapter 5, page 109.***

Sunshine Oil Stove

This delightfully innocent little oil cooker must have been a boon for bedsitters and the like and will add atmosphere to any dolls' house. The good news is, you can make one in minutes.

MATERIALS

Stabilo Boss marker top
Rectangular filigree
    bracelet lozenge
Foil card
    (from takeaway boxes)
Small rectangular frame
Rectangular spacers from
    between bracelet links
Link from a ring chain
Balsa wood
Bead caps x 2
Round-headed pin
Jewellery findings
Butterfly from a
    pierced earring

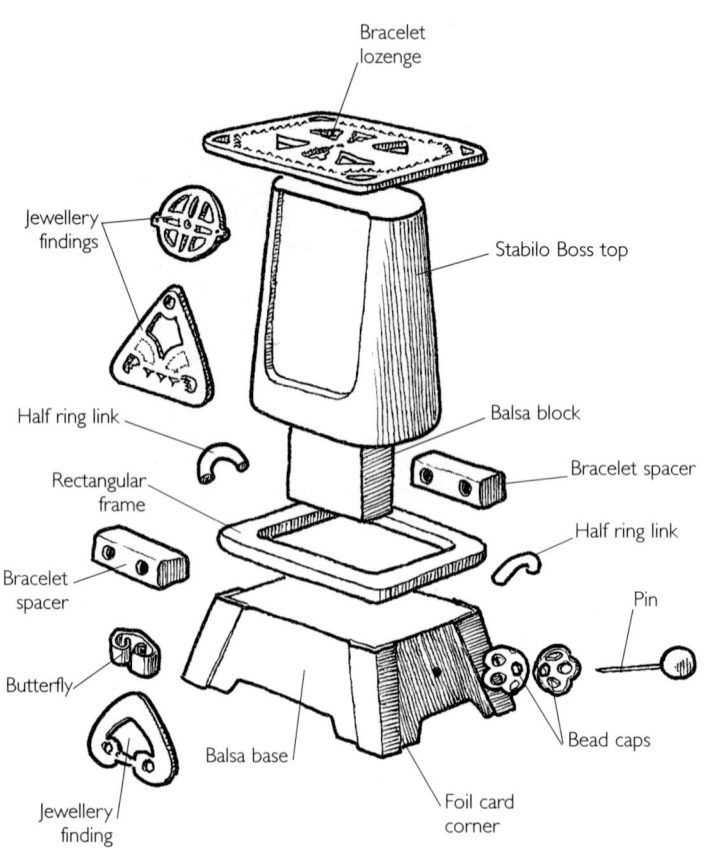

Bracelet lozenge

Jewellery findings

Stabilo Boss top

Half ring link

Balsa block

Rectangular frame

Bracelet spacer

Half ring link

Bracelet spacer

Pin

Butterfly

Bead caps

Jewellery finding

Balsa base

Foil card corner

METHOD

1 Cut a base from balsa, tapering it in on all four sides.
2 Cut a strip of foil card for each corner of the base. Score each down the middle, bend, and bind each corner.
3 Top the base with the rectangular frame.
4 Push the pin through two bead caps and into the side of the base, fixing one of the bead caps to the base and the other just below the head of the pin.
5 Cut a block of balsa to fit inside the marker top. Glue and push the marker top down onto the balsa base.
6 Top the whole assembly with the bracelet lozenge.
7 Decorate the front of the marker top and balsa base with jewellery findings.
8 Cut the ring link in two and use the halves for handles on either side of the base.
9 Add the bracelet spacers to the front and back of the balsa block, and fix the butterfly below the spacer at the front.
10 Spray paint the whole stove silver to finish.

The Gin Genie

'Drink gin and Harpic,' they used to say. 'It will send you right round the bend.' Well, so far I haven't found a use for a Harpic bottle, but a miniature gin bottle provides the basis for a nice stove! Really, almost any small bottle will do. Try adapting the idea to suit the bottles you have. If you have a headache, an aspirin tub works just as well.

MATERIALS

Card
Small plastic bottle
Bell-shaped lid
Metal chain belt lozenge
Belt buckle
Embossed cake
   decoration strip
Felt-tip pen with black casing
   or casing painted black
Square watch case
Bracelet links x 2
Brass washer
Tiny bracelet link
Balsa wood
Plastic Rawlplugs
Beads or decorative
   chain links x 2

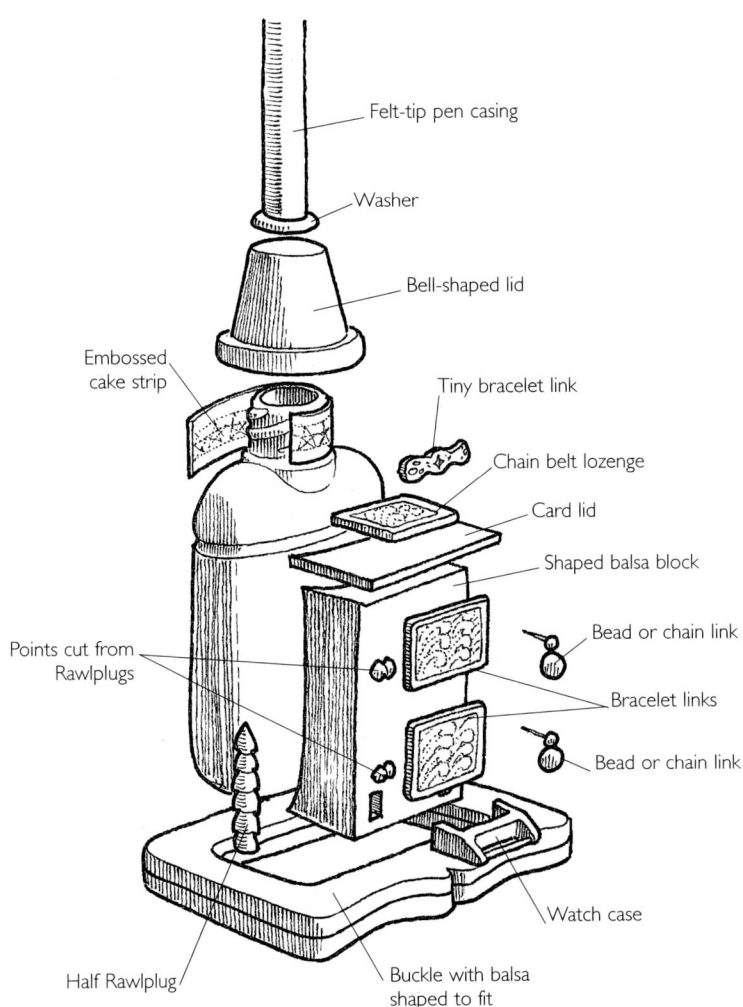

Felt-tip pen casing

Washer

Bell-shaped lid

Embossed
cake strip

Tiny bracelet link

Chain belt lozenge

Card lid

Shaped balsa block

Bead or chain link

Points cut from
Rawlplugs

Bracelet links

Bead or chain link

Half Rawlplug

Buckle with balsa
shaped to fit

Watch case

METHOD

1 Cut a block of balsa for the front, shaping one side of it to fit the bottle.

2 Top the block with a card lid, and decorate the lid with the chain belt lozenge.

3 Arrange two bracelet links on the balsa front for the stove doors.

4 Fix half Rawlplugs at either side of the stove.

5 Add beads or decorative chain links for the door handles and the points cut from Rawlplugs for hinges.

6 Fill in the buckle with balsa, shaped to fit, and glue the stove to this.

7 Cut two holes at the base of the stove front to take the watch case: this forms the ash pan drawer.

8 Hide the screw thread of the bottle neck by wrapping the embossed cake strip around it.

9 Add the makers' nameplate (the tiny bracelet link) to the top.

10 Spray paint the stove black to unite all the parts.

11 Glue the washer to the bell-shaped lid for a chimney holder. Top the stove with this holder, and attach the casing from the felt-tip pen for the chimney.

Mini Peppermint Special

Tasty tic tac peppermints come in a nice, handbag-sized, clear plastic box: 'Just what I need for a free-standing stove', I declared to the world in general as I bought a pack. The girl seemed to be cowering behind the counter and strangely reluctant to take my money. I was right of course; it is just perfect! Well, you know what I mean.

MATERIALS

tic tac box
Long metal lozenge from
    chain belt
Wire mesh
    (e.g. from a bird feeder)
Split pins★ x 4
Jewellery findings
Balsa wood
Card
Wheel from a toy car
Bracelet links x 2
Curtain ring
Long hair slide or brooch

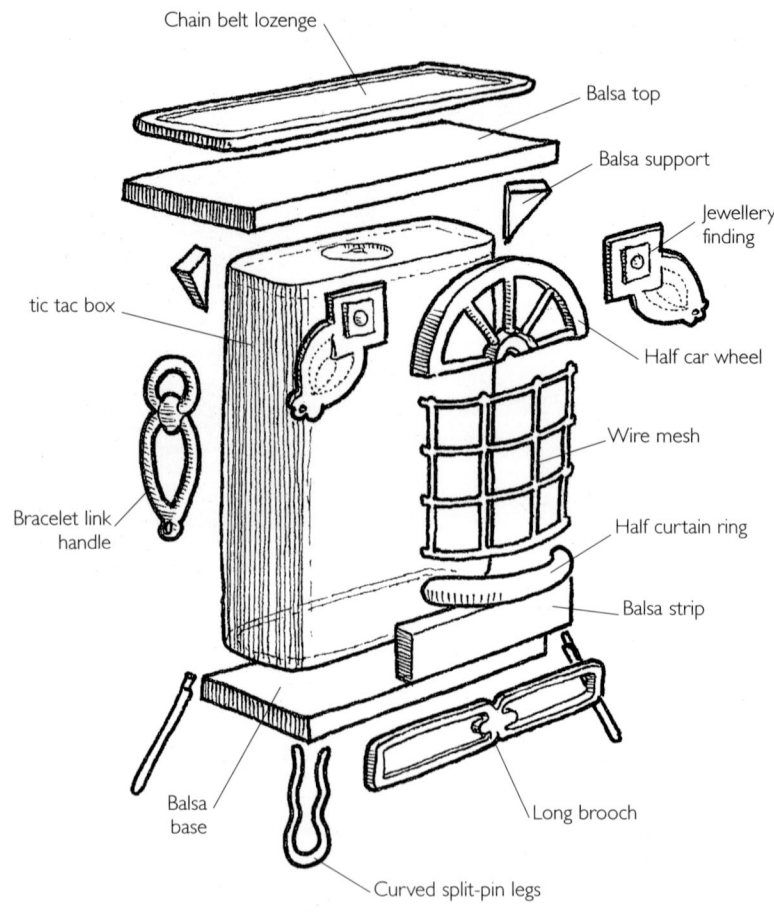

Chain belt lozenge

Balsa top

Balsa support

Jewellery finding

tic tac box

Half car wheel

Wire mesh

Bracelet link handle

Half curtain ring

Balsa strip

Balsa base

Long brooch

Curved split-pin legs

METHOD

1 Cut balsa rectangles for the top and bottom of the stove, making the top slightly larger than the tic tac box all round.

2 Glue the top and bottom in place, and add a chain belt lozenge to the top to give a patterned effect. Use a layer of card to help glue the lozenge in place if necessary.

3 Cut two balsa triangles as supports for the overhanging balsa top.

4 Fix a strip of balsa across the base of the stove.

5 Cut the car wheel in half to use for the top of the stove grill. Cut and slightly bow a piece of mesh for the lower section of the grill, matching up the bars with the wheel.

6 Cut the curtain ring in half and fix it in place as the tray below the grill.

7 Disguise the front edge of the base with the long brooch.

8 Hold the split pins in a vice, and curve them to form the shape of the legs.

9 Glue the bracelet links to either side of the stove, as handles.

10 Decorate the front of the stove, above the grill, with jewellery findings.

11 Mask the grill area, and spray paint the stove gold.

★ YOU MAY BE LUCKY ENOUGH TO FIND THE BRASS PINS THAT WERE THREADED THROUGH THE SHANK OF OLD SHOE BUTTONS: I DID, AND THEY MAKE WONDERFUL LEGS!

The Close Shave Anthracite Stove

My husband little knew what he had started when he sent me into a Boots chemist to pick up a shaving stick. He had, as I remember, specified a certain brand, but from the moment I saw the Boots own brand, he was doomed to use it forever more. I can't vouch for the soap, but the plastic container it comes in is almost a ready-made stove.

MATERIALS

Boots shave stick
Felt-tip pen
Brass cartridge or the lid
    from an eyebrow pencil
Rectangular filigree lozenges
    from metal chain belt or
    bracelet x 2
Smaller bracelet links x 2
Tiny rectangular links from
    metal bracelet
Pierced earrings (studs) x 2
Brooch (a little larger than
    shave stick)
Domed button
Circular bracelet link
Balsa strip
Balsa wood

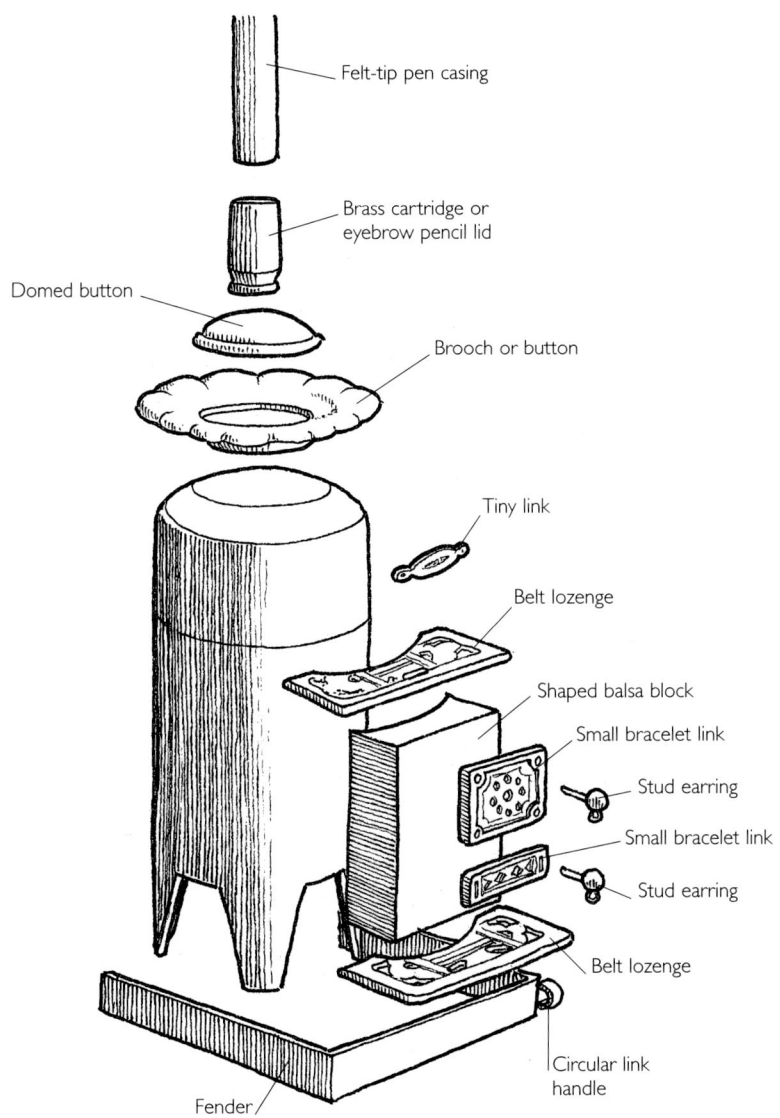

Felt-tip pen casing

Brass cartridge or eyebrow pencil lid

Domed button

Brooch or button

Tiny link

Belt lozenge

Shaped balsa block

Small bracelet link

Stud earring

Small bracelet link

Stud earring

Belt lozenge

Circular link handle

Fender

METHOD

1 Find a brooch a little larger than the top of the shave stick, and glue it in place on the top. Remove any settings and replace them with the button.

2 Cut and shape a block of balsa to fit the lower front of the stove, and glue in place.

3 Fix one rectangular belt lozenge above and one below the balsa block.

4 Open the circular link and fix it to the centre of the bottom link, for a handle.

5 Decorate the front of the block with the smaller links, for fire doors.

6 Add the tiny link to the stove top, above the balsa block.

7 Spray paint the stove black, then spray again with just a dusting of silver.

8 Use a brass cartridge or cut down the brass lid of an eyebrow pencil, and fix it in place on top of the button, to house the stovepipe.

9 Cut the pointed end off the felt-tip pen casing for the stovepipe, and insert it into the brass cartridge on top of the stove.

10 Add the earrings for the door handles.

11 Cut a fender from the balsa strip, score and bend, and spray paint black with a dusting of gold.

CHAPTER 4
PORTABLE HEATERS

Bavarian Schwarz Schwein

The Schwarz Schwein (black pig to you!) was so-called by Hans' niece, Anne Boomsidaisy, who had to stoke it on her visit to Bavaria. She may have been exaggerating when she said it took two tons of anthracite a day . . . you can have a little replica of it without all the drawbacks of the original.

MATERIALS

Salt or pepper pot
Bulgy bead with
  vertical grooves
Rectangular bracelet links x 2
Small bracelet link
Jewellery findings x 3
Long chain link
Plastic mesh from a
  hair curler
Small bottle top
Bead caps x 8
Beads x 3
Watch winder
Wire

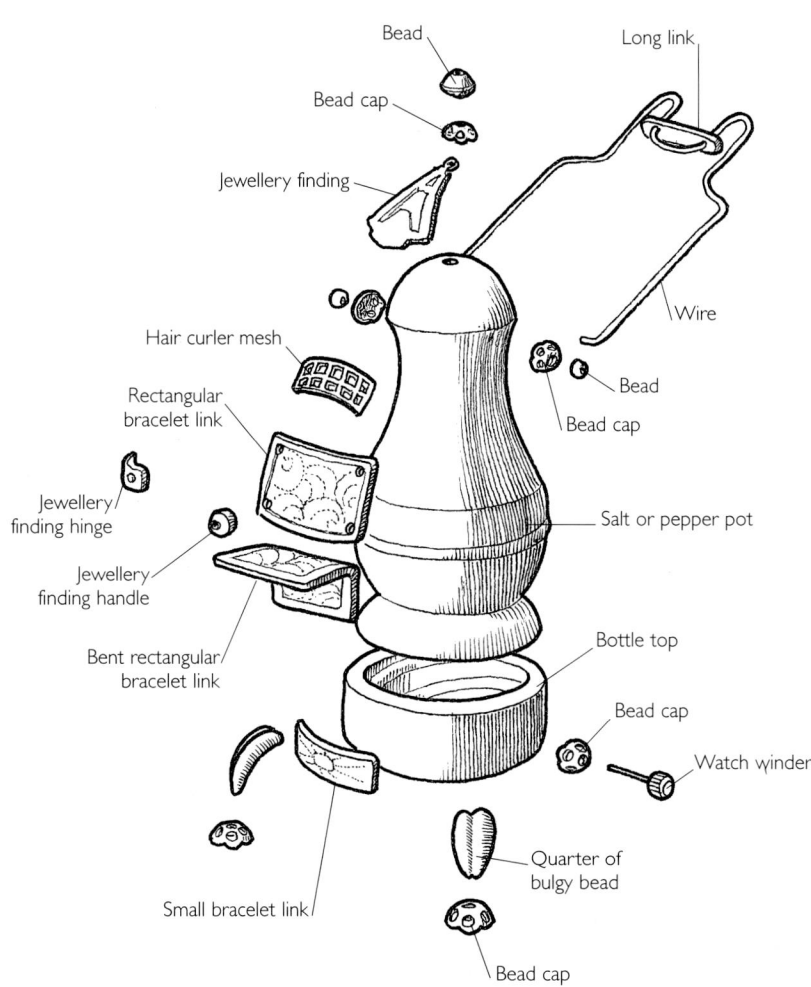

Bead

Long link

Bead cap

Jewellery finding

Wire

Hair curler mesh

Bead

Bead cap

Rectangular
bracelet link

Bead cap

Jewellery
finding hinge

Salt or pepper pot

Jewellery
finding handle

Bent rectangular
bracelet link

Bottle top

Bead cap

Watch winder

Quarter of
bulgy bead

Small bracelet link

Bead cap

METHOD

1 Find a bottle top to fit the base of your salt or pepper pot and glue it in place.

2 Cut the bulgy bead in quarters vertically, and stick each one in a bead cap.

3 Fix these onto the base of the stove as legs.

4 Bend a rectangular bracelet link to take up the curve of the pot.

5 Glue this link, now a door, on the stove front, and add jewellery findings for a hinge and handle.

6 Bend the top half of another bracelet link over (to about 90⁰), and place this to catch ash, below the stove door.

7 Use a small bracelet link for a fire door and attach it to the bottle top.

8 Glue bead caps on either side of the stove, near the top, to take the handle.

9 Thread the wire through the holes of the long link, then bend the wire into a characteristic shape, and inwards at either end.

10 Thread a bead onto each end of the wire, then insert the wire into the bead caps on the pot. Slide the beads along the wire so that they rest against the bead caps.

11 Glue another bead cap to the side of the stove, at the base.

12 Push a watch winder into the central hole of the bead cap and glue it in place.

13 Cut a section from the hair curler mesh to use as a ventilator, and fix it to the top of the pot.

14 Top the pot with a bead set in a bead cap and fix a jewellery finding below this.

15 Spray paint the whole stove dark grey.

Fan Heater

In case you are wondering, this is not a fan heater as we know them today: its name derives from the fact that it is made from a fan. Frankly, I'm a fan fan, and if there is one to be had at a boot sale, I'm the first to swoop on it. In this case you want a fan with blades that are not too wide, and that have only a very small taper, in wood or plastic.

MATERIALS

Identical fan blades x 6
Brooch
Large filigree bead cap
Smaller bead caps x 2
Small rings x 2
Decorative beads x 2
Pin
Medium card
Button
Wire

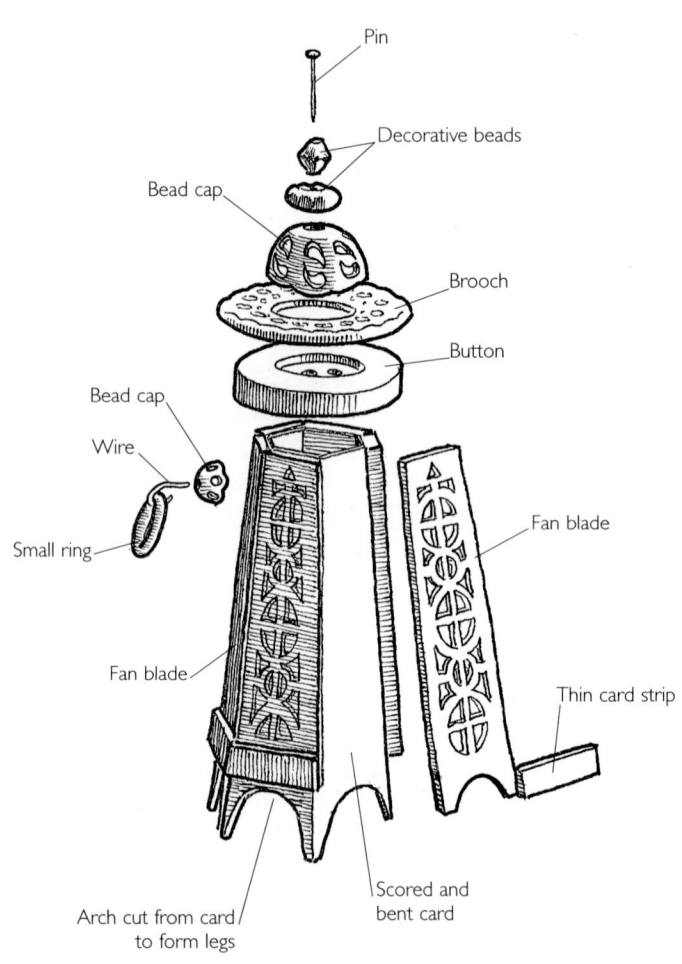

Pin

Decorative beads

Bead cap

Brooch

Button

Bead cap

Wire

Fan blade

Small ring

Fan blade

Thin card strip

Arch cut from card
to form legs

Scored and
bent card

METHOD

1 Lay all six fan blades, the same way up, side by side on a sheet of card, and draw around each of them.
2 Remove the blades, and score along all the vertical lines.
3 Bend the card along these score marks to get the basic stove shape.
4 Cut an arch from the bottom of each section to create legs at each bend.
5 Returning to the fan blades, cut an arch from the bottom of each to correspond with those in the card.
6 Bend the card into a cylinder and glue the edges together.
7 Attach a fan blade to each face of the cylinder.
8 Cut a thin strip of card and band around the base of the cylinder, just above the legs.
9 Top the cylinder with a button, then glue a brooch (having first removed the stone) and a bead cap to this.

10 Thread two decorative beads onto the pin, and stick the pin through the bead cap.
11 Drill a hole near the top of two opposing panels to take the handles.
12 Cut two short lengths of wire. Make the two handles by looping each length through a ring and threading its ends through a bead cap. To position each handle, thread the wire through one of the drilled holes and glue to secure it in place.

The Peking Paraffin Portable

This stove is always popular and it is very adaptable: almost any little cylinder will do as a basis for it. It is so very easy to make.

MATERIALS

Cylinder: lipstick tube or
    cut-down cigar case
Buttons or brooches
    (to fit cylinder) x 2
Additional button or brooch
    or large bead cap and tiny
    gold bead
Embossed cake
    decoration strip
Drop earring
Round-headed pin
Small gold beads x 3
Decorative bead
Wire
Bead caps x 3
Long chain link
Jewellery finding

92

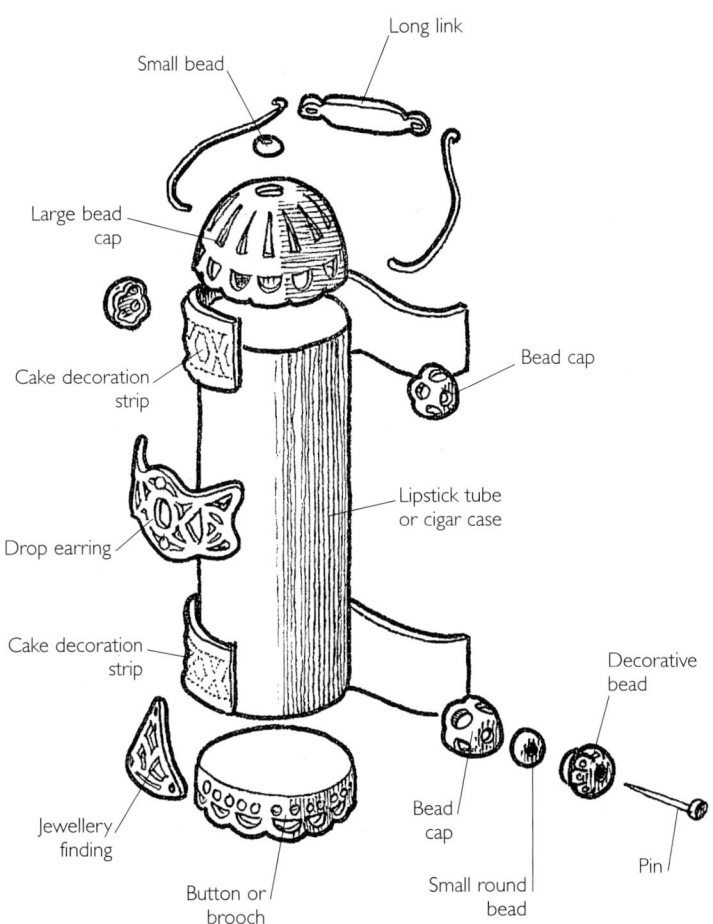

Long link

Small bead

Large bead cap

Cake decoration strip

Bead cap

Drop earring

Lipstick tube or cigar case

Cake decoration strip

Decorative bead

Jewellery finding

Bead cap

Pin

Button or brooch

Small round bead

METHOD

1 Find a button or brooch to fit the cylinder. If you are using a brooch, remove any stones. Stand the cylinder on this base and glue the two together.

2 Now you must decide whether you want a flat or a domed top. For a flat top add a button or a brooch. For a domed top, add a large bead cap, upside down, topped with a small bead. (A domed top is illustrated.)

3 Bind around the top and bottom of the cylinder with a narrow band of cake decoration strip.

4 Add a jewellery finding to the banding around the base.

5 Use a drop earring for the door, removing any stones from the setting. Bend the earring frame round to fit the curve of the cylinder.

6 Bore a pin hole through the side of the cylinder, at the base. Insert a pin through a decorative bead, a small round bead and a bead cap, then stick the pin through the hole.

7 Slide the bead cap down the pin to rest on the side of the cylinder, and slide the two beads along to the other end of the pin. Fix in place.

8 Thread one long or two short lengths of wire through the holes in the long link, then bend the wire into a characteristic handle shape.

9 Drill holes in the sides of the cylinder to take the handle.

10 Thread each end of the wire through a bead cap, before gluing the handle in place.

11 Spray paint gold.

Hugh Wood True Valor 'C'

It's not often a stove becomes so popular they write a hymn in its praise, but of course we have all heard of this one. (Though the next line, 'Let him come hither', does puzzle me a bit.)

MATERIALS

Brass lipstick case
Large round brooch
Small round brooch
Pierced earring butterfly
Embossed cake
   decoration strip
Bead caps x 2
   (one slightly smaller than
   the other)
Watch case
Vitamin bottle lid
Flat buttons x 2
   (one slightly smaller than
   the other)
Pin
Small beads x 5 (4 matching)
Small jewellery finding
Decorative bead

METHOD

1 Pile up and glue, in this order, the larger button, the bottle lid and the smaller button. Follow these with the lipstick case and watch case, then the large round brooch, the decorative bead and finally, the pierced earring butterfly.

2 Band around the lipstick case, under the watch case, with a cut-down section of cake decoration strip.

3 Glue the smaller brooch in the centre of the lipstick case as a door.

4 Add a small jewellery finding to the front of the bottle lid as a makers' nameplate.

5 Drill a hole into the side of the bottle lid.

6 Thread a pin through a small bead and bead cap, followed by a larger bead cap, then insert the pin into the hole in the bottle lid.

7 Mount the stove on four small bead feet.

8 Spray paint the stove silver.

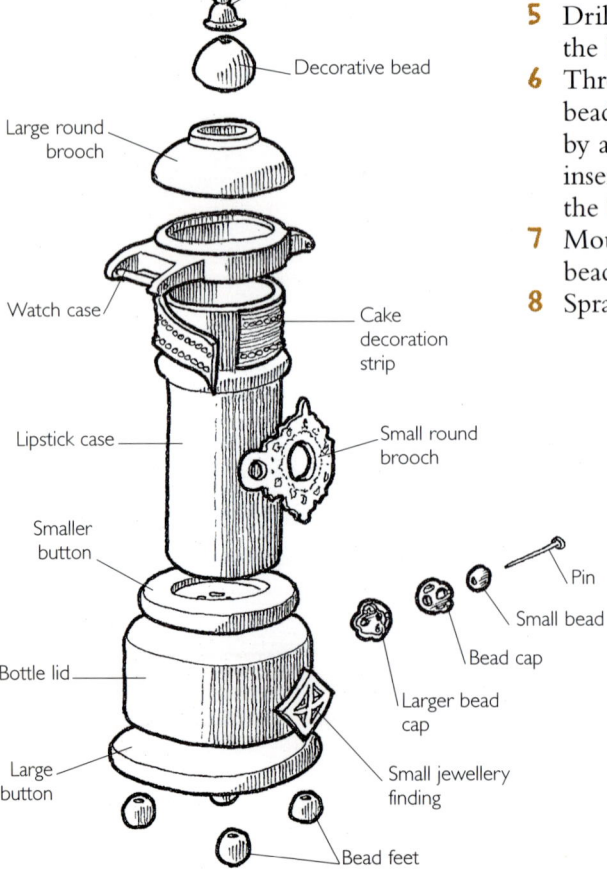

Butterfly

Decorative bead

Large round brooch

Watch case

Lipstick case

Smaller button

Bottle lid

Large button

Cake decoration strip

Small round brooch

Pin

Small bead

Bead cap

Larger bead cap

Small jewellery finding

Bead feet

Fancy Coal Hod

MATERIALS

Firm card
Light card
Rectangular metal
    bracelet link
Round-headed pin
Belt rivets x 2
Tiny ring

METHOD

Draw two side pieces and a long panel (for the central piece), following the diagram. Cut the two side pieces from firm card and the long piece from light card. Score across the long piece so you can fold it and glue the resulting, oddly-shaped box between the side panels. Decorate the front of the box with the metal bracelet link. Fix the ring between two rivets for the carrying handle, and insert the pin below the bracelet link for the door handle. Spray paint brown.

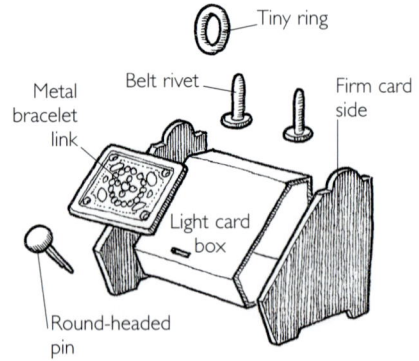

Tiny ring

Belt rivet

Firm card side

Metal bracelet link

Light card box

Round-headed pin

Upright Coal Hod

MATERIALS

Cigar case
Button
Brass wire
Bead caps x 2
Eye from hook and eye
Long chain link (optional)

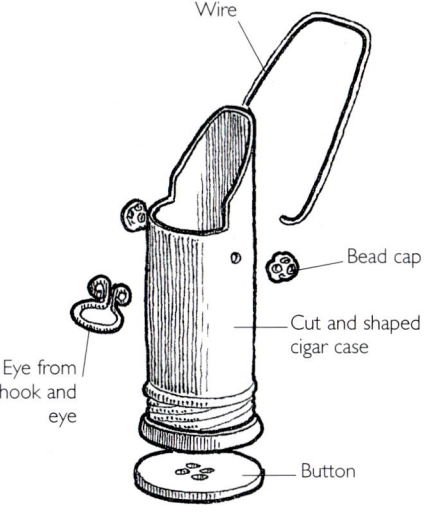

Wire

Bead cap

Cut and shaped
cigar case

Eye from
hook and
eye

Button

METHOD

Cut the cigar case 2¾ in (70mm) up from the lid, leaving the lid on, and shape the lip. Make a hole on either side of the lip to take the handle. Mount the cigar case on a button base. Bend a length of wire into a handle shape. Alternatively, before bending the wire, thread it through a long chain link to provide a grip. Thread each end through a bead cap and then through the cigar case. Fix the bead caps over the holes. Bend the centre of the eye (from the hook and eye) forward and glue it to the front of the coal hod. Spray paint gold.

Low Coal Hod

MATERIALS

Cigar case
Collar stud
Brass paper fastener
Fancy bracelet link

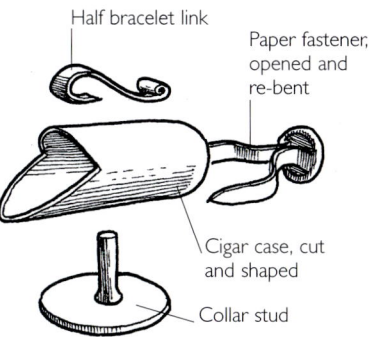

Half bracelet link

Paper fastener, opened and re-bent

Cigar case, cut and shaped

Collar stud

METHOD

Cut the cigar case 1½ in (40mm) from the rounded end, and shape the lip. Cut the hinged bar away from the collar stud and use it as a stand for the hod. Open up the paper fastener and rebend as shown, before gluing it over the rounded end of the cigar case. Cut the fancy bracelet link in half and glue it in place as a handle. Spray paint gold.

Dinky Fire Irons

METHOD

STAND

Bend back four points on the flower bead cap to make hanging hooks for the fire irons. Thread a length of brass wire through a bead, then mount the flower bead cap on the bead. Replace the stone from the brooch with a second bead and thread the other end of the wire through this. Glue in position.

MATERIALS

STAND
Brass wire
Beads x 2
Bead cap
Flower bead cap
Brooch with stone setting

FIRE IRONS
Brass wire
Small beads x 2
Small bead caps x 3
Pipe cleaner
Tiny rings x 2
Brass shim
Small screw eye
Small rings (from a chain) x 4

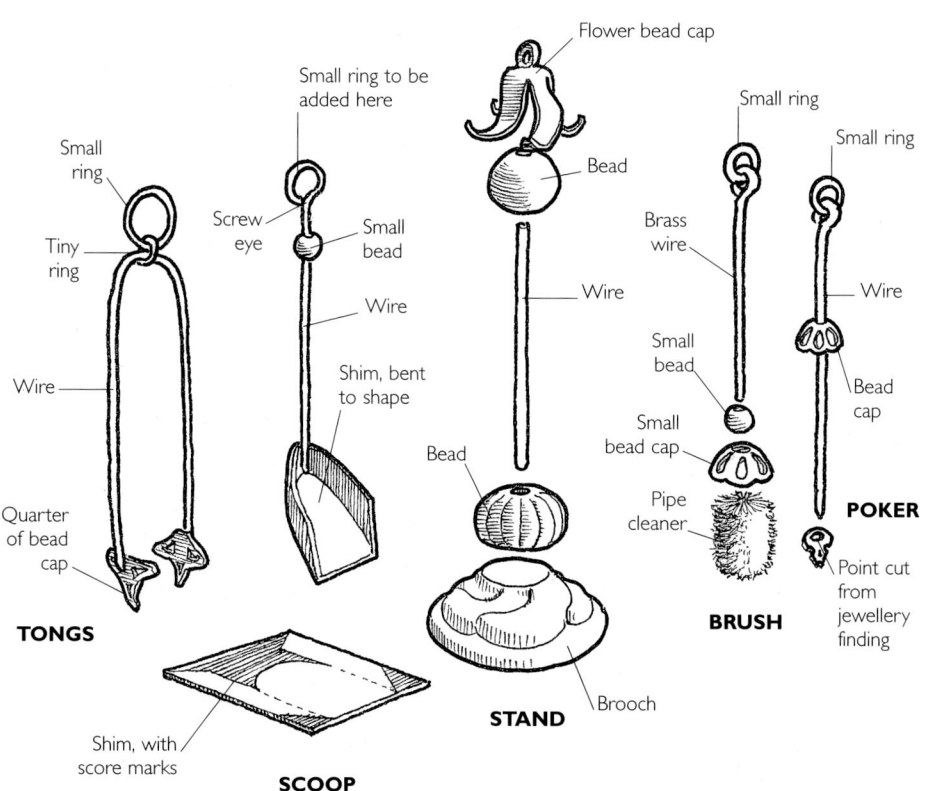

Flower bead cap

Small ring to be
added here

Small ring

Small ring

Small
ring

Bead

Screw
eye

Small
bead

Brass
wire

Wire

Tiny
ring

Wire

Wire

Small
bead

Shim, bent
to shape

Bead

Wire

Small
bead cap

Bead
cap

Quarter
of bead
cap

Small
bead cap

Pipe
cleaner

POKER

TONGS

BRUSH

Point cut
from
jewellery
finding

Shim, with
score marks

Brooch

STAND

SCOOP

103

FIRE IRONS

For the brush, thread a length of wire through a small bead and bead cap. Fix these at one end of the wire, and bend the other end into a hook. Cut a small section of pipe cleaner and glue this into the bead cap. The scoop is made from shim. Score and bend a small piece, cutting a little nick at the back so that you can bend it up and glue it to a length of wire. Fix a small bead to the other end of the wire, and insert a screw eye in the top of the bead. To make the poker, bend a length of wire into a tiny ring at one end and add a bead cap halfway down. Finish with a little point cut from a jewellery finding. For the tongs, thread a fourth length of wire through a tiny ring, and bend the wire into the required shape. Stick a quarter of a bead cap to each end. Add a small ring to the top of each tool, and hang them on the stand.

Fancy Fireguard

MATERIALS

Toy zoo railing
  x 3 sections
Leatherette
  (e.g. from an old diary)
Rectangular lozenges from
  chain belt x 2
Long bracelet links x 2
Necklace clasp
Firm card
Narrow bangle
Cocktail sticks x 4

METHOD

Straighten out the bangle, then rebend it to the shape of a fender. Trace around this fender onto card and cut out three pieces of card to this shape: one for the base, one for the top, and one for the leather seat. Cut one section of railing down to half height, removing any 'bobbles'. Use the other two sections full height, cutting off any ornamentation from the top, to flank this middle piece. Line the bangle with one of the card shapes, and arrange the railing to fit it by bending it round at the

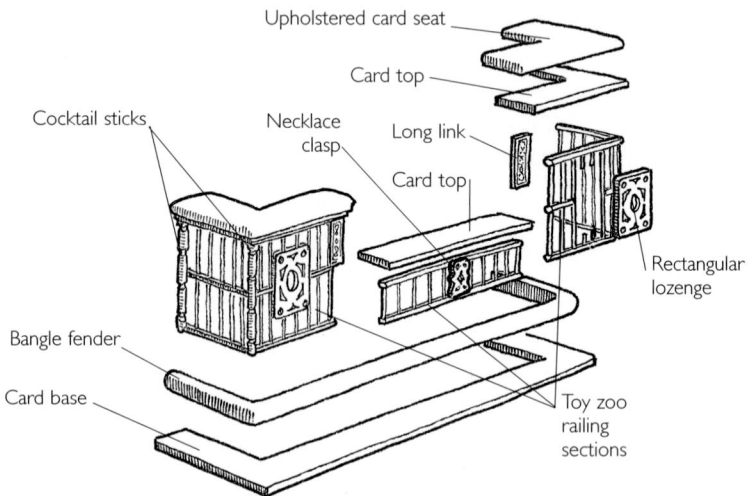

Upholstered card seat

Card top

Cocktail sticks

Necklace clasp

Long link

Card top

Bangle fender

Card base

Rectangular lozenge

Toy zoo railing sections

sides. Reinforce the ends and corners of the railing with cocktail sticks. Place the two rectangular lozenges behind the sections of full-height railing, and cut away any rails that cross them. Fix in place. Fit the top piece of card by cutting away the middle section to fit the half-height fence. Reinforce the inner sides of the railing with the two long links, and add the necklace clasp to the centre front.

For the seat, cut out the middle section from the remaining card shape, and upholster the two outside pieces with the Leatherette. Spray paint the fireguard brown before sticking the upholstered seats to the top rails.

Accessories

Many accessories can be easily made from whatever findings you have to hand. A few are listed below to give you some ideas.

Brassware

Any small, brass-coloured findings can be 'glued together' to create different brassware pieces. Useful findings include: buttons, bracelet links, bead caps, beads, brass wire, toy bells and earrings.

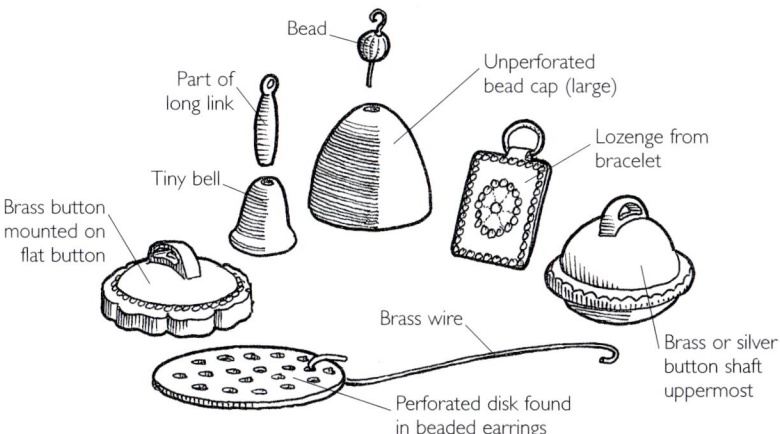

Ornaments

Mount animals and figures from charm bracelets or Christmas crackers on buttons and brooches. Glue small beads and bead caps together to make 'miscellaneous' decorative pieces.

Charms from charm bracelets

Small diamanté buckle

Bead caps

Bead

Flat ovals from a bracelet

Pots and Pans

Brass olives can be used as they are for pots and pans, topped with shank buttons for lids. Long links and eyes from hook and eye fasteners make instant handles. Cut and bend brass shim or mesh for scoops and spatulas. Miniature bottles are available commercially.

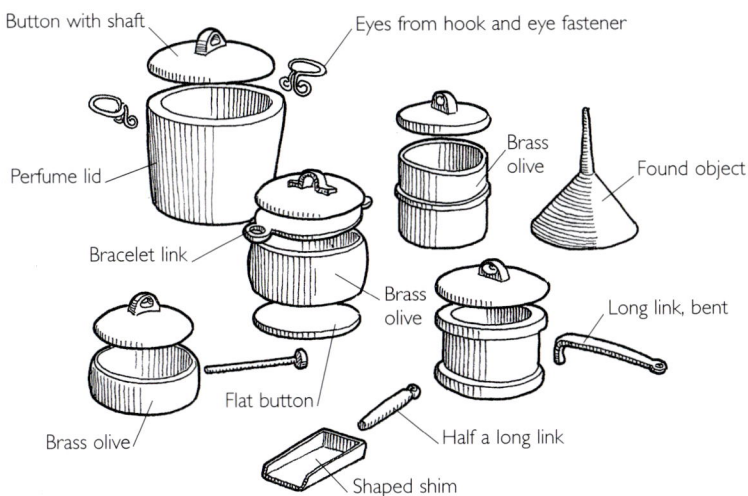

Button with shaft

Eyes from hook and eye fastener

Brass olive

Found object

Perfume lid

Bracelet link

Brass olive

Long link, bent

Flat button

Brass olive

Half a long link

Shaped shim

109

Vases

Insert a tiny piece of oasis into a perfume bottle lid and add small, dried flowers, or use a brass cartridge case as a vase.

Tiny dried flowers

Brass cartridge case

Oasis

Lipstick base

Candlesticks

Thread beads and bead spacers onto a pin, starting and finishing with a bead cap.

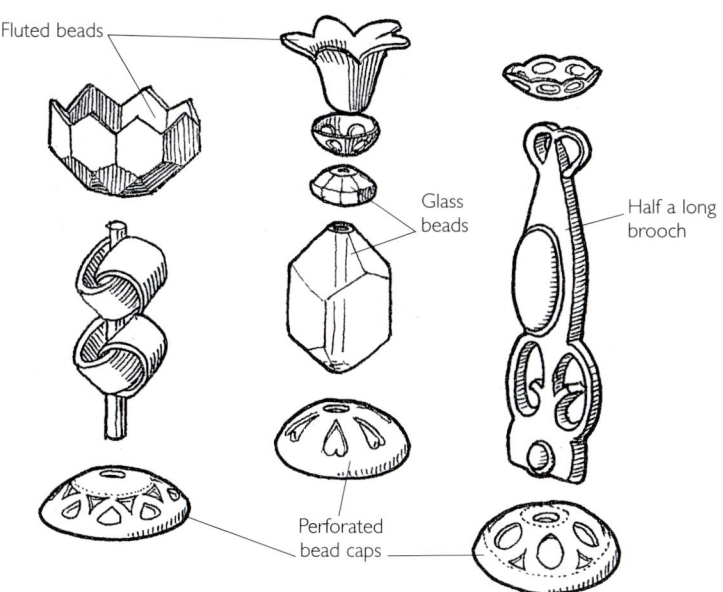

Fluted beads

Glass beads

Half a long brooch

Perforated bead caps

Mantel Clocks

Cut out small illustrations of clock or watch faces from catalogues and mount them on earrings or brooches. Make sure the faces are photographed straight-on, or your model will appear distorted. For a domed glass case, cut down a test tube.

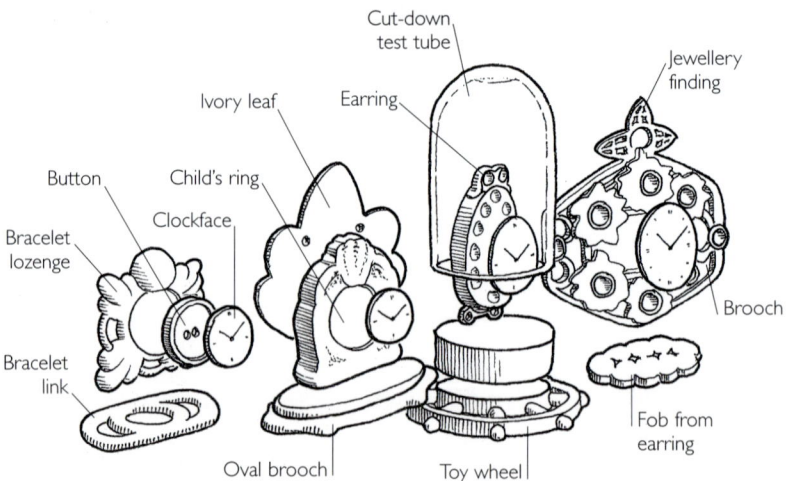

Framed Photos and Paintings

Cut out any small pictures that take your fancy, and trim them to fit inside brooches, earring drops, and other jewellery findings. Stick a long link or collar stud to the back for a stand.

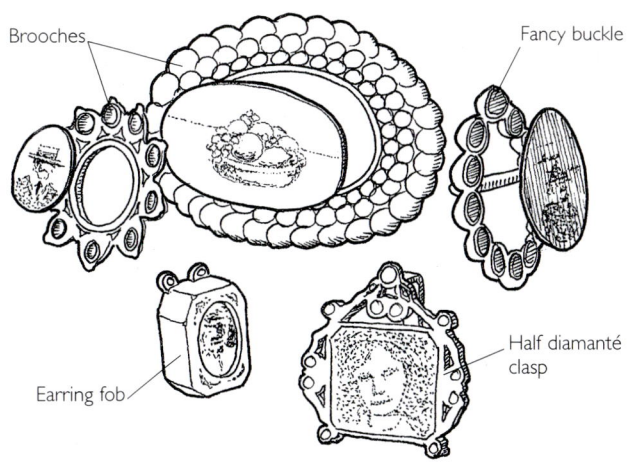

Brooches

Fancy buckle

Earring fob

Half diamanté clasp

Fireguards

Decorative fireguards can be made with filigree brooches and buckles, using flattened bead caps or links cut in half for legs. Whatever gives the look you want, use it.

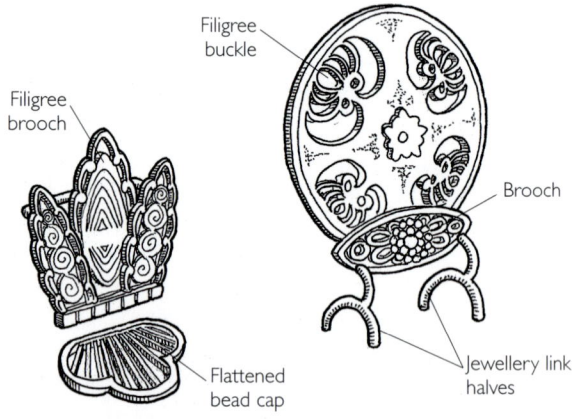

Filigree buckle

Filigree brooch

Brooch

Flattened bead cap

Jewellery link halves

About the Author

Patricia King went to a progressive school which valued individual enterprise. She then studied stage design at art school, going on from there to design backgrounds for windows at a London store.

When her children started school, she took a teaching qualification and taught at colleges of further education for more years than she will ever admit.

Now retired, she has more time for the painting, potting and crafts she used to teach. Her husband makes and runs a model railway so they share a love for scale model making. She attributes an enduring relationship to the fact that they both have their own sheds as hobby areas and therefore hardly ever see each other! They have, however, found time to have a thriving family of children and grandchildren who are all creative.

Patricia discovered dolls' housing while in the USA, where she lived for three years. Making dolls' house furniture was a natural hobby for her to take up, and since starting to write articles and books on the subject, she is amazed to find how many wonderful people there are, all over the world, who are on the same wavelength.

VIDEOS

MAGAZINES

Woodturning • Woodcarving • Furniture & Cabinetmaking
The Router • The ScrollSaw • The Dolls' House Magazine
Creative Crafts for the home • BusinessMatters

The above represents a list of related titles currently published or scheduled to be published. All are available direct from the Publishers or through bookshops, newsagents and specialist retailers. To place an order, or to obtain a complete catalogue, contact:

GMC Publications
Castle Place, 166 High Street, Lewes, East Sussex BN7 1XU, United Kingdom
Tel: 01273 488005 Fax: 01273 478606

Orders by credit card are accepted